In Their Place

Radical Geography

Series Editors:
Kate Derickson, Danny Dorling
and Jenny Pickerill

Also available:

Space Invaders
Radical Geographies of Protest
Paul Routledge

In Their Place

The Imagined Geographies of Poverty

Stephen Crossley

www.plutobooks.com

First published 2017 by Pluto Press
345 Archway Road, London N6 5AA

www.plutobooks.com

British Library Cataloguing in Publication Data
A catalogue record for this book is available from the British Library

ISBN   978 0 7453 3683 1   Hardback
ISBN   978 0 7453 3679 4   Paperback
ISBN   978 1 7868 0119 7   PDF eBook
ISBN   978 1 7868 0121 0   Kindle eBook
ISBN   978 1 7868 0120 3   EPUB eBook

This book is printed on paper suitable for recycling and made from fully
managed and sustained forest sources. Logging, pulping and manufacturing
processes are expected to conform to the environmental standards of the
country of origin.

Typeset by Stanford DTP Services, Northampton, England

Simultaneously printed in the United Kingdom and United States of America

Contents

Contents

For Harriet, Daisy and Sam.
I hope I make you proud.

Acknowledgements

The idea of a sole-authored book is, in this instance at least, a misnomer. Whilst the majority of the words that follow are mine, the ideas on which they are based, and the work on which they hopefully build, are not. Although relatively few people have been directly involved in helping me write this book, many more have been supportive of me in my wider writing endeavours and in helping me think through and develop some of the ideas contained within these pages. There are too many of these people to mention individually here but, hopefully, you know who you are. If in doubt, ask me next time you see me.

My PhD supervisors Roger Smith and Lena Dominelli have given me the confidence, freedom and time to write this book when really I should have been concentrating on my thesis. Thank you. Jenny Thatcher and her colleagues of the British Sociological Association Bourdieu Study Group kindly invited me to give a paper at an event they held in November 2014, which encouraged me to explore the 'through the front door' rhetoric associated with the Troubled Families Programme, discussed in Chapters 7 and 8. I believe Tracey Jensen must take some of the blame/credit for suggesting me. Sadie Parr also kindly invited me to submit an article to *People, Policy and Place* online, which enabled me to clarify and formalise some of my thinking around changing state forms and interventions – and this was also very helpful preparation for Chapter 7. Dan Silver's photographic reminders about the symbolic power of abandoned shopping trolleys reassured me that this issue 'was a thing'.

In tracing the events that led to me submitting a proposal for the Radical Geography series, I must thank Jane, John, Adrian, John again, Tom, Ted, Linda, Ted again, and Danny. The views of the three anonymous reviewers were very helpful in shaping the final manuscript. New colleagues at Northumbria University have helped protect me from the potential ravages of entering employment as a university lecturer in the current period. Special thanks go to Lucy, Claire, Marion, Justine, Sean, Alison and John, who have been very supportive and protective of me, helping me to find time to write, although I'm not sure many were aware of just what I was doing when I kept telling them I was busy.

Danny Dorling, surely a contender for nicest man in academia, has been incredibly supportive and approachable since the day I first met him. Being told by him that he thought we shared the same prejudices remains a career highlight. His comments on drafts of the chapters have undoubtedly added to the book. Maggie Walker and Ian Menter also helped to make sure the final version was a lot more incisive than my first attempts. David Castle at Pluto has been consistently supportive and helpful, and patient. And Neda's e-mails always made me smile, so thank you as well.

Special mention must go to Tom Slater and Gerry Mooney, whose critical interrogations of place and space, and the ways in which spaces can be deployed and used against marginalised groups, have been so useful to me. I returned to them many times when I was struggling with my writing. But more than that, they have both been very consistent supporters of me, and my other scholarly efforts. I would like them to know that their messages and offers of support mean a lot to me.

Finally, Mam, Dad and Jo, thank you for everything.

Series Preface

The Radical Geography series consists of accessible books which use geographical perspectives to understand issues of social and political concern. These short books include critiques of existing government policies and alternatives to staid ways of thinking about our societies. They feature stories of radical social and political activism, guides to achieving change, and arguments about why we need to think differently on many contemporary issues if we are to live better together on this planet.

A geographical perspective involves seeing the connections within and between places, as well as considering the role of space and scale to develop a new and better understanding of current problems. Written largely by academic geographers, books in the series deliberately target issues of political, environmental and social concern. The series showcases clear explications of geographical approaches to social problems, and it has a particular interest in action currently being undertaken to achieve positive change that is radical, achievable, real and relevant.

The target audience ranges from undergraduates to experienced scholars, as well as from activists to conventional policy-makers, but these books are also for people interested in the world who do not already have a radical outlook and who want to be engaged and informed by a short, well written and thought-provoking book.

Kate Derickson, Danny Dorling and Jenny Pickerill
Series Editors

1
Introduction
The Spaces of Others

The idea of difference is at the basis of the very notion of space, that is, a set of distinct and coexisting positions which are exterior to one another and which are defined in relation to one another through relations of proximity, vicinity, or distance, as well as through order relations, such as above, below, or between.

Pierre Bourdieu, 1996.[1]

THE OTHERS

Space has been called 'the fundamental stuff of geography',[2] and many influential geographers such as Henri Lefebvre, Doreen Massey, David Sibley and Edward Soja have written extensively on the importance of space and the ways in which it is socially produced and reproduced, shaping and being shaped by our relations with each other. By way of example, in her book *For Space*, Doreen Massey articulated three 'opening propositions': space is the product of interrelations and is constituted through interactions, whether global or intimate; space is the sphere of possibility and represents multiplicity, heterogeneity and plurality – a site where individual trajectories co-exist; and space is always under construction, never finished and never closed.[3] There is, then, general agreement that the concept of space as a dead, fixed and immobile place is no longer relevant. Massey stated in *For Space* that it may therefore be productive to think about space differently. This book attempts to think differently about the spaces associated with people living in poverty. There is, however, no grand narrative, or meta-theory being advanced here. Instead, the intention is to draw attention to the ways in which various groups of people, such as politicians, academics, policymakers, journalists and social reformers use spaces in different ways, doing so, more or less explicitly, to support and augment their arguments and perspectives on poverty.

The alleged behavioural failings and moral inferiority of people living in poverty have attracted a great deal of academic and political scrutiny over the course of the last 400 to 500 years. Researchers have argued that the conflation of poverty with criminality can be traced back to 'the happy sixteenth-century custom of chopping off the ears of vagabonds, rogues and sturdy beggars'.[4] Other issues such as poor parenting, drug addiction, a less than enthusiastic approach to work, sexual promiscuity and poor financial management have also been advanced as causes or 'drivers' of poverty on a fairly regular basis. These insinuations are examples of how people experiencing poverty are Othered by the rest of society, or those who do not experience such hardship. In this way, the alleged behaviour of 'the poor' help to establish them as a distinct group, a separate social entity different and inferior to 'the non-poor'. Othering has been described as:

A dualistic process of differentiation and demarcation, by which the line is drawn between 'them' and 'us' – between the more and the less powerful – and through which social distance is established and maintained. It is not a neutral line for it is imbued with negative value judgments that construct 'the poor' variously as a source of moral contamination, a threat, an 'undeserving' economic burden, an object of pity or even as an exotic species.[5]

Baroness Lister, who has written extensively about poverty and the negative representations of people living on low-incomes, describes Othering as a 'discursive strategy that magnifies and distorts difference' and one that has material effects on poor people.[6] How we refer to people, the names or labels we attach to them, has implications not just for how they are treated by wider society, including its institutions, but also for how those labelled see themselves. Importantly, when powerful groups such as politicians and/or policymakers name something or attach a label to a group, it removes the right or the ability of that group to name and define themselves. The French anthropologist Colette Petonnet, in her book *Those People*, a study of residents of a French public housing project she called La Halle, highlighted how:

Lumped together under the same scorn and sadly surprised by the names they are called, the residents of La Halle have no alternative but to recognise themselves as the group they form in relation to the outside world.[7]

A contemporary example of the labelling of disadvantaged groups, that also has a long history, can be found in the UK government's Troubled Families Programme. Following riots that broke out in England in 2011, David Cameron, the then prime minister, sought to blame the disturbances on a small hard-core group of trouble-making families. He launched the Troubled Families Programme shortly afterwards and said:

> Let me be clear what I mean by this phrase. Officialdom might call them 'families with multiple disadvantages'. Some in the press might call them 'neighbours from hell'. Whatever you call them, we've known for years that a relatively small number of families are the source of a large proportion of the problems in society. Drug addiction. Alcohol abuse. Crime. A culture of disruption and irresponsibility that cascades through generations.[8]

Cameron used research that estimated there were around 120,000 families that experienced 'multiple disadvantages' such as poverty, material deprivation, maternal mental health issues, and poor housing in 2004/5 to support his case that there were the exact same number of families involved in crime, anti-social behaviour, truancy from school and where at least one parent was in receipt of out-of-work benefits in 2011.[9]

Labels similar to 'troubled families' have been around since Victorian times when there was a concern about a 'social residuum' and a 'submerged tenth' of the population. The desire to split 'the poor' into 'deserving' and 'undeserving' groups can be traced back to the 1834 Poor Law. Since then, the belief that there is an 'underclass' in British society, cut off from the rest of 'us' and displaying different norms, values and customs, has been recycled on a fairly frequent basis, with slight changes in emphasis or labels at different times.[10] Not all of these labels have received 'official' status from the government, but many have captured the imagination of the wider population. Viewing some people living in poverty as a 'threat' to wider society has obvious implications not just for the types of policies that are developed to address poverty, but also for the media headlines that are generated in discussions about poverty and the type of support that is offered to such groups.

The process of Othering people living in poverty and of recycling and reconstructing the 'underclass' thesis has continued in spite of a lack of empirical evidence and over a century's worth of academic research in the UK that suggests that structural and political issues such as low pay, a lack of good quality jobs and low levels of state support for those people out of work are, and pretty much always have been, the main causes of poverty.[11]

In addition to the causes of poverty, spatial inequalities in the concentration of poverty are also well documented, dating all the way back to Charles Booth's colour-coded poverty maps of London in the 1880s and 1890s. Today, colour-coded, computer-generated 'heat maps' of the UK are often used to highlight the poverty and other assorted problems faced by deindustrialised areas in England's north-east and north-west, and along the 'M62 corridor' between Leeds and Manchester. Poor neighbourhoods have also been extensively researched, with a long history of ethnographic studies, where the researcher immerses themself in the daily life of a district and its inhabitants, on both sides of the Atlantic and beyond. Friedrich Engels, the German philosopher who worked closely with Karl Marx, famously spent nearly three years living in Manchester in the 1840s and published an account of his observations and experiences in *The Condition of the Working Class in England* in 1844. From the 1920s onwards, sociologists and students from 'the Chicago School' have been encouraged to view their city as a 'living laboratory'. The sheer output of many of these researchers, keen to 'better understand' the daily lives of 'the poor' or 'the disadvantaged' sometimes gives the impression that the streets of poor or 'deprived' neighbourhoods are crammed full of sociologists, geographers and anthropologists lurking on street corners, undertaking participant observation.[12]

Researchers are, of course, not the only non-residents with an interest in these areas. In Victorian times, London's middle classes went 'slumming' – visiting the poorer East End of London – for a variety of reasons, including for entertainment purposes as well as for research, philanthropic and charitable reasons, an interest that has been recreated in a recent BBC television series called *The Victorian Slum*. Journalists were some of the most active 'slummers', often going in search of good copy and keen to tell tales of debauchery and depravity. Contemporary newspaper reports of 'ghettos of welfare scroungers' and the investigative journalist Donal MacIntyre's 'exposé' of street mugging in Brixton suggest that some things never change.[13] Visits by politicians and their 'special' advisors to poor neighbourhoods are often used as the political setting for, or precursor to, speeches, policy announcements or think-tank reports about poverty and how best to address it. These visits, and the political rhetoric that accompanies them, purport to 'tell it like it is', with the politicians keen to be able to claim that they have seen the effects of poverty 'first-hand' and 'with their own eyes'. And yet, almost without exception, the political (and media) construction of these neighbourhoods, and their residents, ends with them being at least partially blamed, more or less subtly, for the problems associated with them.

Such visits are part of a longer history of the discrediting of entire neighbourhoods, helping to portray them as 'dreadful enclosures' or 'phantasms, which feed on emotional experiences stimulated by more or less uncontrolled words and images'.[14] The geographer David Sibley, in his book *Geographies of Exclusion*, noted that this history of 'imaginary geographies' helps to cast minority groups as threatening Others and 'polluting bodies or folk devils who are then located elsewhere'.[15] Parts of the East End of London, for example, were likened to 'darkest Africa' and its inhabitants likened to pygmies and 'wandering tribes' in Victorian times. The American sociologist E.V. Walter, who attempted to expose 'the myth of the dreadful enclosure', wrote in 1977 that:

> In all parts of the world, some urban spaces are identified totally with danger, pain and chaos. The idea of dreadful space is probably as old as settled societies, and anyone familiar with the records of human fantasy, literary or clinical, will not dispute a suggestion that the recesses of the mind conceal primeval feelings that respond with ease to the message: 'Beware that place: untold evils lurk behind the walls'. Cursed ground, forbidden forests, haunted houses are still universally recognised symbols, but after secularisation and urbanisation, the public expression of magical thinking limits the experience of menacing space to physical and emotional dangers.[16]

More recently, the concept of 'territorial stigmatisation', which draws attention to the way in which urban areas and neighbourhoods can come to be associated with problematic groups and behaviour, has been advanced by the urban sociologist Loïc Wacquant.[17] He, like Walter and others before him, highlights the way that impoverished areas can become 'spatially tainted' by political and media discourses linking them with a wide range of social problems. The stigmatisation of an entire local area ensures that its residents are presented as a homogeneous group and tarred with the same brush. Wacquant reels off a list of neighbourhoods across different countries which are synonymous with disorder and deprivation:

> In every metropolis of the First World, one or more towns, districts or concentrations of public housing are publicly known and recognised as those urban hellholes in which violence, vice, and dereliction are the order of things. Some even acquire the status of national eponym for all the evils and dangers now believed to afflict the dualised city: Les Minguettes and La Courneuve or the Mirail housing complex in Toulouse for France; South Central Los Angeles, the Bronx and the project of Cabrini Green in Chicago for the United States; Duisberg-Marxloh and Berlin-Neukölln for Germany; the districts of Toxteth in Liverpool, Saint Pauls in Bristol, or Meadow Well in Newcastle for England; and Bijlmer and Westlijke Tuinsteden in Amsterdam for Holland ... Whether or not these areas are in fact dilapidated and dangerous, and their population composed essentially of poor people, minorities and foreigners, matters little in the end: the prejudicial belief that they are suffices to set off socially noxious consequences.[18]

The concept of territorial stigmatisation, which is discussed in more detail in Chapter 4, 'spotlights space as a distinctive anchor of social discredit'.[19] Wacquant, in developing the concept, drew on Pierre Bourdieu's concept of 'symbolic power' and melded it with Erving Goffman's influential work on stigma. Goffman, who has been called the most influential American sociologist of the twentieth century, wrote about the ways in which people attempt to manage their 'spoiled identities' when they fail to live up to other people's standards in an effort to avoid social discredit. Bourdieu, perhaps the most influential sociologist of the last 50 years, described symbolic power as the 'power to construct reality',[20] a 'power of creating things with words' and 'a power of consecration or revelation, a power to conceal or reveal things which are already there'.[21] Bourdieu argued that this power to bring things to life was available to certain people who had earned or were granted the authority to talk about things as if they were experts, such as politicians, journalists, academics and others in positions of power. These people could use this power to shape other people's perceptions about the world, creating a 'vision of divisions', as he called it.[22] Bourdieu also used the concept of 'symbolic violence' to highlight forms of soft, coercive power, which are often used against people with their consent, or 'the violence that is exercised upon a social agent with his or her complicity'.[23]

THE IMAGINED GEOGRAPHIES OF OTHERS

Despite the Othering of people living in poverty being extensively documented, and places of poverty, most notably disadvantaged neighbourhoods, being sites of a great deal of political and academic scrutiny, many spatial aspects of Othering have remained, by comparison, relatively unresearched. There are, however, some obvious exceptions. In *Orientalism*, the Palestinian public intellectual and professor of literature, Edward Said noted that:

> A group of people living on a few acres of land will set up boundaries between their land and its immediate surroundings and the territory beyond, which they call 'the land of the barbarians'. In other words, this universal practice of designating in one's mind a familiar space which is 'ours' and an unfamiliar space beyond 'ours' which is 'theirs' is a way of making geographical distinctions that *can be* entirely arbitrary.[24]

Said argued that discourses circulating about objects and places did not result in a 'delivered presence, but a *re-presence*, or a representation', which often relied little on reality and 'excluded, displaced, [and] made supererogatory any such *real thing* as "the Orient"'.[25] There were 'supreme fictions' that portrayed people and cultures of 'the East' as inferior and more primitive than allegedly more civilised Western societies. Although his focus was on the way that the West 'exoticised' Oriental Others via this discourse, his arguments and observations carry similar weight when examining how 'the non-poor' represent 'the poor', and the idea of representations of spaces will be returned to throughout this book. Said highlighted that there was a 'large mass of writers', including

> poets, novelists, philosophers, political theorists, economists and imperial administrators [that] have accepted the basic distinction between East and West as the starting point for elaborate theories, epics, novels, social descriptions, and political accounts concerning the Orient, its people, customs, 'mind', destiny, and so on.[26]

Whilst highlighting the strength of the discourse surrounding the idea of the Orient and the fact that men (*sic*) not only made their own history but also their geography, Said argued that although the Orient was 'essentially an idea', it was not 'a creation with no corresponding reality'.[27] Thus, the spaces and places of the Orient existed, as do poor neighbourhoods and other spaces inhabited or frequented by 'the poor' that are discussed in this book, but the representations of these places by powerful people do not necessarily reflect the 'reality' of them. In another important point that is relevant to the discussion in this book, Said argued that 'ideas, cultures, and histories cannot seriously be understood or studied without their force, or more precisely their configurations of power, also being studied'.[28] Discourses about the Orient were, he believed, 'something more formidable than a mere collection of lies' and that their 'sheer knitted-together strength' needed to be understood and respected. A large part of this discursive strength came from the 'very close ties to the enabling socio-economic and political institutions, and its redoubtable durability'.[29]

Said argued that every space was, in some way, linked to another one and that there were no totally 'isolated' or 'pure' spaces, or spaces that were not 'represented' in some way. In a similar vein, the Canadian sociologist Rob Shields argues in his book *Places on the Margin*, that:

> marginal places that are of interest are not necessarily on the geographical peripheries but, first and foremost, they have been placed on the periphery of cultural systems of space in which places are ranked relative to each other. They all carry the image, and stigma, of their marginality which becomes indistinguishable from any basic empirical identity they might once have had.[30]

Thus, it is often the cultural properties associated with spaces, and representations of these spaces, that marks them out as different or marginalised, rather than the physical location, properties or empirical realities of the spaces themselves. A third example of a work that examines aspects of spatial Othering is David Sibley's seminal book *Geographies of Exclusion*, mentioned above, which begins with the statement that 'the human landscape can be read as a landscape of exclusion'.[31] Sibley attempted to 'foreground the more opaque instances of exclusion' that are taken for granted and accepted as part of everyday life, and highlighted the implicit forms of inclusion and exclusion that exist in the design and use of space.[32] Sibley's work highlighted the symbolic importance of boundaries, liminal spaces, 'imagined geographies' and 'clean spaces', free from 'polluting populations'.[33] He believed it was 'necessary to examine the assumptions about inclusion and exclusion which are implicit in the design of spaces and places'[34] and suggested that 'the boundary question' – the 'sense of border between self and other' – was a 'traditional but very much under-theorised concern in human geography'.[35]

The ways in which everyday, mundane spaces such as the front door of the family home, 'the house(hold)', the street corner, the local shops and the local school, are symbolically constructed, and how they can contribute to the Othering of people living in poverty has not attracted as much attention or comment. These taken-for-granted spaces have all been put to use in different ways by politicians and media commentators, not to mention researchers, yet they should not be regarded as mere backdrops to the alleged deviant or problematic behaviour of people living on low incomes. Just as the putative behaviour, habits and customs of disadvantaged communities and populations have been used to create distinctions between 'us' and 'them', so have the 'imagined geographies' used, traversed and inhabited by such groups. People living in poverty are expected to be found, or indeed kept, in certain places and, by extension, they also face symbolic and material exclusion from occupying or moving through other spaces.

This book, then, intends to examine how spaces and spatial metaphors are deployed in discourses that circulate about people living on the margins of our society and, more specifically, those that live in poverty. It aims to highlight how various 'imagined geographies' associated with poor populations are brought to life by people in positions of power. These symbolically potent spaces and boundaries help to Other 'the poor' and bring them to life in the minds of 'the non-poor'. They strengthen political discourses surrounding poor individuals, families and communities. Such images and metaphors can be used to keep or 'fix' people in their place, to exclude them from other spaces and thus make sure that people living in poverty *know* their place.

A quick and contemporary example to demonstrate how local, everyday spaces can create distinctions and draw a line between 'them' and 'us', thus helping construct our views on reality, can be found in a statement made by the then chancellor of the exchequer in the UK, George Osborne. In a section of his speech to the Conservative Party conference in 2012, Osborne talked about fairness in the welfare state, and rhetorically asked:

> Where is the fairness, we ask, for the shift-worker, leaving home in the dark hours of the early morning, who looks up at the closed blinds of their next door neighbour sleeping off a life on benefits?[36]

This single sentence manages to bring imagined people and spaces, and their relationship to each other, to life. The exact details of the images in people's heads may differ, but everyone listening to the speech or reading about it afterwards is encouraged to imagine a member of a 'hardworking family', who crosses the symbolic threshold of the family home in the cold, dark hours of the early morning to go out to work. In the house next door, according to Osborne, his neighbour lies snuggled up in bed, lazily enjoying the trappings of a life paid for by other people's taxes and with something to hide, or be ashamed of, behind closed blinds.

The use of the term 'shift-worker' implies unrewarding and repetitive work. The 'look up at the closed blinds' suggests that he or she is annoyed at the unfairness of their neighbour being asleep at this time. The safety and security of a bedroom is contrasted with the cold, dark outside. The social distance between the two people mentioned is in stark contrast to the physical proximity: this is a 'striver' living not just on the same street as a skiver, but right next door to them. This proximity is important in attempts to create a 'vision of divisions'. Living next door to someone 'sleeping off a life on benefits' must, we are encouraged to think, be much harder than being aware of these people existing in some far-off estate in another part of town. Familiarity breeds contempt.

Pierre Bourdieu suggested that '[t]he preconstructed is everywhere'[37] and that it was necessary for sociologists and other critical scholars to break with common-sense views and widely used classificatory systems. He urged social researchers to reject the opportunity to simply ratify the social problems that the state presented them with, including 'false oppositions' such as 'deserving' and 'undeserving' poor, and engage in research that can 'twist the stick in the other direction'[38] and think differently about the world. Bourdieu, in taking his own advice, often took as his subject 'precisely those attitudes, dispositions, and ways of perceiving reality that are taken for granted by members of a social class or a society'.[39]

Whilst geographers have not been particularly quick to embrace his significant body of work,[40] there are a number of elements of it that help to underpin the approach adopted here. Bourdieu believed that the task of sociology was to 'help reveal what is hidden',[41] and he also believed that tangible, observable phenomena often served to obscure less tangible structures and forces which helped to shape social life.

> Interactions, which bring immediate gratification to those with empiricist dispositions – they can be observed, recorded, filmed, in sum, they are tangible, one can 'reach out and touch them' – mask the structures that are realised in them. This is one of those cases where the visible, that which is immediately given, hides the invisible which determines it. One thus forgets that the truth of any interaction is never entirely to be found within the interaction as it avails itself for observation.[42]

The argument that visible phenomena cannot provide the whole truth of any situation is a key point for this book. Seeing poverty, or the places where poor people live, with one's own eyes is not the same as seeing everything relating to poverty, or indeed seeing the things that matter in attempting to address it. Observing the effects of poverty in certain places, or talking about them in certain settings, does not necessarily lead to a better understanding of the causes of poverty and can, in some cases, mask the less tangible forces that prevent people from acquiring an adequate income and standard of living, leading to 'common-sense' views about people experiencing poverty. Bourdieu called this *doxa*, the taken for granted view of the world, where alternative or competing discourses remain largely undiscussed.[43]

Bourdieu argues that we cannot hope to understand the reality of 'what is lived and seen *on the ground*' by attempting to see things 'first-hand' in deprived neighbourhoods.[44] Instead, he argues that the reality is to be found elsewhere, using American ghettos to highlight the fact that state services in these districts have been withdrawn and 'rolled back', leaving behind 'abandoned sites that are fundamentally defined by an *absence*'.[45] Like Sibley, Massey and other geographers, Bourdieu writes about ways in which space can be produced and dominated by powerful groups, prompting us to think about the way the state decides on regeneration and housing schemes, which areas are identified as 'sink estates' suitable only for demolition, which get 'regenerated' with new housing, and how much of any new housing is termed 'affordable'. His observation that the consumption of space is one of the most important ways that power can be used and displayed helps us to think about similar contemporary issues, including the 'bedroom tax' which means that social housing tenants in the UK cannot receive support for a 'spare' bedroom in their property. It also highlights the ways in which affluent people are able to consume completely different spaces not just residentially, but in a number of everyday practices and locations, such as first-class travel, private health care and schooling, and 'VIP only' areas in nightclubs. The introduction of 'poor doors' in parts of the USA and the UK, where social housing tenants are provided with separate entrances to apartment blocks to keep them away from private owners who can access their apartments via a 'luxury lobby' is perhaps one of the most insidious ways in which space is dominated and consumed differently, depending on income. As Bourdieu noted, 'socially distanced people find nothing more intolerable than physical proximity'.[46]

The work of Bourdieu, Sibley, Wacquant, Lister and others, then, offers up possibilities for examining and scrutinising the construction of the spaces of people living in poverty: the 'different worlds' that people living in poverty inhabit; the 'no-go' areas where 'teenagers rampage around the estate' and where it is 'standard for children to have a mum and not a dad'; the street corners and liquor stores where poor, black Americans 'hang out' or sell drugs; the 'failing schools' that disadvantaged children attend; and the front rooms of 'troubled families' with their flat-screen TVs, empty pizza boxes and 'sofas of despair'.[47]

Whilst all of these spaces appear natural and are often taken for granted in popular discourses, we should not underestimate the amount of work that goes into 'creating' them and making them appear this way. Identifying these spaces as the sites of problems faced by people living in poverty also helps to deflect attention away from other sites, where these representations are created, as Bourdieu noted.

> The perfectly commendable wish to go see things in person, close up, sometimes leads people to search for the explanatory principles of observed realities where they are not to be found (not all of them, in any case), namely at the site of observation itself. The truth about what happens in the 'problem suburbs' certainly does not lie in these usually forgotten sites that leap into the headlines from time to time. The true object of analysis, which must be constructed against appearances and

against all those who do no more than endorse those appearances, is the social (or more precisely political) construction of reality as it appears, to intuition, and of its journalistic, bureaucratic and political representations, which help to produce effects that are indeed real, beginning with the political world, where they structure discussion.[48]

Shifts in emphasis towards or away from certain spaces in media and political discourses are also accompanied by a shift in the space(s) where state intervention is proposed – as Murray Edelman has remarked in an examination of the symbolic uses of politics, 'there are no neutral spaces'.[49] If politicians want to highlight the need for a programme of neighbourhood renewal, they can make a visit to a poor disadvantaged area to emphasise the point. If, however, the policy focus is to be on 'troubled families', great play can be made of the need for workers to 'get in through the front door' of the family home so that they can work with them 'from the inside out'. Winning support for reforms to the education system that focus on the performance and capability of individual schools can be achieved by talking about 'failing schools' where 'you can smell the sense of defeatism', as Michael Gove, the former UK education secretary did when discussing schools in east Durham, a deprived former mining area in the north-east of England.[50] Rhetoric that focuses on such localised, everyday spaces thus draws attention away from the sites of political decisions affecting these areas, and also away from the backgrounds of those making the decisions.

The remainder of the book examines some of the different spaces and places linked with poverty and poor populations that are constructed and brought to life by people in positions of authority and power. Many of the constructions and descriptions of these places have been articulated by affluent and privileged white men, in occupations such as politics, research and journalism. This is not because their voices are more worthy than others, but because their voices have been more powerful and more influential than others, and it is this group that have traditionally been involved in creating representations of impoverished groups. People living in poverty are rarely involved in articulating their own needs and aspirations, often because more powerful Others feel very capable of speaking on their behalf. This is a point made by David Sibley in *Geographies of Exclusion* where he highlights how the voices of people from certain cultures and geographies have been systematically marginalised by white Westerners.[51]

Space, however, if the pun can be excused, prevents us from discussing every possible location, real or imagined, that is invoked in discourses surrounding people and places and poverty. Chapter 2 examines the way in which poor people have been portrayed as an 'exotic species' or as 'internal aliens' over the last 100 years by people making comparisons with outposts of Empire, developing countries and magical spaces such as 'twilight worlds'. In Chapter 3, attention turns to the portrayal of deindustrialised 'decaying' cities and the people that live in them. This discussion then turns to how more economically successful cities attempt to exclude marginalised people from 'polluting' the spaces of consumption in city centres, keeping them 'purified' and 'vibrant'. Chapter 4 examines the depiction of poor neighbourhoods as, for example, 'sink estates' and 'dreadful enclosures', and suggests that 'Westminster effects' on the people living in these areas are stronger than more usually researched 'neighbourhood effects'. The focus in Chapter 5 is 'the street', examining the history of street sociologists and criminologists in the UK and the USA and attempting to problematise concepts such as the 'code of the streets', 'street capital' and 'street government' that have been advanced in recent years. Chapter 6 focuses on 'the household', a key unit in anti-poverty policies, but one which receives relatively little critical scrutiny from policymakers or researchers. Assumptions about dynamics within the household are unpicked, and the exclusion from poverty figures of groups that do not fit neatly into household categories is highlighted. Chapter 7 crosses the symbolic threshold of the front door and examines the way that internal spaces such as bedrooms, kitchens and front rooms have been portrayed in historical and contemporary discourses about poor families. Bureaucratic spaces such as jobcentres, children's centres, housing offices and libraries are discussed in Chapter 8, including an examination of the shifting spaces of the new neoliberal state. The final chapter summarises the points made in the preceding chapters, highlighting the ways in which public and private spaces are constructed and then used to construct different policy responses. The book ends by arguing that it is time we looked elsewhere, in less researched territories, if we want to really understand how and why poverty continues to exist in the twenty-first century.

2

Swamps and Slums

Exoticising the Poor

Two nations between whom there is no intercourse and no sympathy; who are as ignorant of each other's habits, thoughts, and feelings, as if they were dwellers in different zones, or inhabitants of different planets: who are formed by a different breeding, are fed by different food, are ordered by different manners, and are not governed by the same laws.

Benjamin Disraeli, 1845.[1]

Contemporary concerns about the 'dangers' to poorly defined concepts such as 'British values' and a 'British way of life' posed by migrant communities and 'foreigners' in general highlight how potent the image of the 'exotic' Other can be. This 'Orientalist' view of the world is inextricably linked to ideas about the superiority of Western civilisation and the simplistic deployment of damaging and problematic stereotypes when discussing citizens of Asian, North African and Middle Eastern countries, as highlighted by Edward Said.[2] Such views lead to media and political discourses around 'bogus asylum seekers', 'swarms of immigrants' coming to the UK to take advantage of our benefits system, and towns being 'swamped' by migrant workers and foreign nationals.

These views about 'exotic Others' have, at various points throughout history, elided with domestic discourses about what might be called more 'familiar Others' – people living in poverty in the UK, and also in the United States, resulting in what has been called 'domestic colonialism'.[3] This chapter sets out how, from Victorian times through to the current day, there have been numerous attempts, using spatial metaphors and imaginary geographies, to depict those living on low incomes and living in disadvantaged neighbourhoods as being of a different and inferior race or breed. Where Benedict Anderson, an eminent historian and political scientist, famously asserted that nations were 'imagined communities',[4] here we see communities as 'imagined nations'.

In Victorian times, the exotic imagery used to depict poor populations was undoubtedly more explicit and forthright than today, and there was undoubtedly more of it. Domestic poverty and outposts of empire were often mixed up, and much social commentary on the lot of the poor in the late nineteenth century was a mixture of social fact and exotic fiction. In the 1960s, the development of the idea of a culture of poverty, first 'observed' by the cultural anthropologist Oscar Lewis in a number of small scale studies carried out in Latin American countries, was imported into the United States by the journalist Michael Harrington, who (mis)used the concept in his influential book *The Other America* (see below).[5] Fast forwarding to more recent times, we can hear echoes of Harrington's concern about a 'second America' and 'an invisible land' that the middle classes are unaware of in the 'broken Britain' discourses promulgated by the think tank the Centre for Social Justice and other 'spontaneous sociologists', the name Bourdieu gave to people immediately available for media comment on any social issue.[6] The chapter ends with a short discussion which suggests that, whilst the language used in contemporary discourses may be slightly subtler, traces of the historical narratives which exoticise people living in poverty in the UK can still be found.

'DARKEST ENGLAND'

In the Victorian era, members of the middle classes who went 'slumming' were feted as social 'explorers' and the practice was often intertwined with reflection on Britain's imperialism, with the East End of London often symbolically 'doubling' as an outpost of the British Empire.[7] These comparisons managed to pathologise not only the inhabitants of poor neighbourhoods in London, but also those inhabitants of other countries 'lucky' enough to be visited by British explorers. The East End was referred to as 'the dark continent', and imagery of 'wild races', 'wandering tribes', 'savages', 'street arabs' and 'pygmies' living in foul and fetid 'swamps' and in 'the jungle' were often invoked by early 'explorers'.[8] Henry Mayhew, author of *London Labour and the London Poor* (1851), argued that when passing from the West End of London to the East End, it was 'as if we were in a new land, and among another race'.[9] Journalists who went slumming in search of good copy claimed that they were going 'Haroun Al Raschid', paying respect to an eighth-century caliph who had gone undercover as a poor man in order to better understand the conditions and daily lives of his subjects.[10] University settlements, where young students and graduates from Oxford and Cambridge would live and work in poor neighbourhoods for short periods of time, were set up as a form of residential 'colony'.[11] Mrs Henrietta Barnett, the wife of Samuel Barnett who established the Toynbee Hall settlement,[12] wrote that a lady who had visited, 'expressed great astonishment to find that the people lived in houses' as she had 'expected that they abode, not exactly in tents, but in huts ... or squatted against a wall'.[13]

There are numerous other examples of such views. The novelist Walter Besant described the East End as a 'region of London which is less known to Englishmen than if it were situated in the wildest part of Colorado, or amongst the pine forests of British Columbia'.[14] James Greenwood, who wrote *The Wilds of London* (1874) and was one of the first journalists to bring to light the plight of workhouse inmates in the Victorian era, likened the men he slept alongside in the workhouse to the '"brutes" he had read about in "books of African travel"' and was 'intrigued by what he called "curiosities of savage life"'.[15] A few years later, in 1883, George Sims, an English poet, journalist, dramatist and novelist, began his book *How the Poor Live* by inviting the reader to go on a journey with him, not across oceans or land but 'into a region which lies at our own doors – into a dark continent that is within easy walking distance of the General Post Office'.[16] Sims hoped that this continent would be:

As interesting as any of those newly-explored lands which engage the attention of the Royal Geographic Society – the wild races who inhabit it will, I trust, gain public sympathy as easily as those savage tribes for whose benefit the Missionary Societies never cease to appeal for funds.

Perhaps the most extensive articulation of this 'domestic colonialism' – the merging of the 'primitives' and 'savages' 'discovered' in the far flung corners of the British Empire and the condition of the working classes at home – came from William Booth, the founder of the Salvation Army.[17] Drawing on the poverty maps of London developed by his namesake Charles Booth, as well as his own experiences, William Booth argued that the residents of the slums of Britain were best viewed in the same light as the pygmies found in 'darkest Africa'. He urged the readers of his book, *Darkest England, and the Way Out*, to attempt to understand the size, not to mention the danger, of the jungles that were being traversed by explorers such as Henry Morton Stanley:

> The immensity of wooded wilderness, covering a territory half as large again as the whole of France, where the rays of sun never penetrate, where in the dark, dank air, filled with the steam of the heated morass, human beings dwarfed into pygmies and brutalised into cannibals lurk and live to die.[18]

Booth stated that there were two kinds of pygmies: the first type was 'a very degraded specimen with ferretlike eyes' who was more akin to a baboon than he thought possible, but was still 'very human'; and the other type was 'very handsome, with frank open innocent features'.[19] He acknowledged that the picture he painted was 'terrible', but he went on to write that he could not help but see similarities between the sights allegedly encountered by visitors to Africa and those who stayed closer to home:

> As there is a darkest Africa, is there not also a darkest England? Civilisation, which can breed its own barbarians, does it not also breed its own pygmies? May we not find a parallel at our own doors, and discover within a stone's throw of our cathedrals and palaces similar horrors to those which Stanley has found existing in the great Equatorial forest? [...] The more the mind dwells upon the subject, the closer the analogy appears. The ivory raiders who brutally traffic in the unfortunate denizens of the forest glades, what are they but the publicans who flourish on the weakness of our poor. The two tribes of savages, the human baboon and the handsome dwarf, who will not speak lest it impeded him in his task, may be accepted as the two varieties who are continually present with us – the vicious, lazy lout and the toiling slave.[20]

Booth continued in similar vein, arguing that, 'The foul and fetid breath of our slums is almost as poisonous as that of the African swamp'.[21] His proposed solution to the domestic situation he described was voluntary emigration for the 'submerged tenth' of the population who lived in such conditions, to a 'colony over-sea' where colonists, freed from their depraved environment would be educated in 'honesty, truth and industry'.[22] It was, he concluded, and drawing parallels with explorers such as Stanley once again, 'necessary to organise rescue expeditions to free the miserable wanderers from their captivity, and bring them out into the larger liberty and the fuller life'.[23]

It should be noted that Booth, despite apparently travelling over 60,000 miles during 60 years of ministry, never actually visited Central (or 'darkest') Africa as Stanley had.[24] Booth made it as far as the United States, Canada, Australia and South Africa, but not to anywhere which was in the process of being 'discovered' by British explorers. Stanley faced extensive criticism for his racism and for the fierce and physical treatment of the Africans he encountered on his explorations, including those whom he employed. There were numerous contemporary accounts of him and his men killing Africans with little explanation or provocation, and plundering their possessions.[25]

William Booth was writing in 1890, and it would, one might hope, be easy to dismiss his and his contemporaries' rhetoric as a relic of another time, a darker and less enlightened period, if you will. But traces of Booth's writing live on in more recent and even in contemporary debates about the living conditions and lifestyles of the working classes and those living in poverty. The evacuation of children from urban neigh-bourhoods during the Second World War brought the prevalence and effects of poverty into full view of the rural middle classes who had been previously ignorant of such conditions. A highly influential report by the Women's Group on Public Welfare called *Our Towns* argued that the appearance of young children evacuated from slums in the 1940s served as proof that the 'submerged tenth' that both Charles and William Booth wrote about could still be found over 50 years later.[26] Just as William Booth drew parallels between the 'vicious louts' and 'toiling slaves' he saw in East London and the African pygmies from another place, the report of the Women's Group on Public Welfare made links between the 'dull and backward' children of the 1940s with those of Booth's investiga-tions, from another time. The report also noted that the slums of Britain were 'widespread and a source of shock and scandal to fellow-citizens of the Empire',[27] suggesting that conditions were worse at home than in other countries.

THE OTHER AMERICA

In 1962, a journalist named Michael Harrington published a book exposing the extent of poverty in the United States, providing an explicit example of Othering people living in poverty. The book, *The Other America*, drew heavily on Oscar Lewis's controversial theory of a 'culture of poverty', although Lewis thought that his concept had been misunderstood by Harrington. Lewis himself acknowledged that 'the phrase [a culture of poverty] is a catchy one and has become widely used and misused', adding that Harrington had used the phrase 'in a somewhat broader and less technical sense than I had intended.'[28] Notwithstanding this concern, Harrington's book was to become one of the most influential texts in the development of the US government's 'war on poverty', which ultimately petered out because the war in Vietnam was afforded political and financial primacy. Harrington wrote in evocative prose about this 'other America', and in the first chapter described how poverty remained hidden in what he called the 'invisible land':

> Poverty is off the beaten track. It always has been. The ordinary tourist never left the main highway, and today he rides interstate turnpikes. He does not go into the valleys of Pennsylvania where the towns look like movie sets of Wales in the thirties.[29]

Poor young people did not 'disturb the quiet streets of the middle class',[30] and, due to increasing suburbanisation in the countryside, poor communities were no longer 'just across the tracks'.[31] The increasing physical separation between the American middle and working classes thus neatly served as a metaphor for the cultural decoupling that Harrington wanted to articulate. Suggesting that poor communities no longer shared in the 'American Dream', he went on to say that the other America 'does not contain the adventurous seeking a new life and land'.[32] This situation, Harrington argued, had gone largely unnoticed because 'there are enough poor people in the United States to constitute a subculture of misery, but not enough of them to challenge the conscience and the imagination of the nation'.[33] Depicting poor, working class people as inhabitants of 'anachronistic spaces', Harrington argued that 'these are the people who are immune to progress'.[34] His description of them as 'internal aliens', growing up in 'a culture that is radically different from the one that dominates the society' emphasises this view that the other Americans were stuck in their ways, out of place and out of time.[35]

In the concluding chapter of his book, Harrington continued this theme:

At the same time, the United States contains an underdeveloped nation, a culture of poverty. Its inhabitants do not suffer the extreme privation of the peasants of Asia or the tribesmen of Africa, yet the mechanism of misery is similar. They are beyond history, beyond progress, sunk in a paralyzing, maiming routine.[36]

Although he sought to make a distinction between American poverty and the poverty experienced in other parts of the world, he argued that 'the misery was similar'.[37] Three pages later, he argued that the causes were the same as well, and that 'like the Asian peasant, the impoverished American tends to see life as a fate [sic], an endless cycle from which there is no deliverance'.[38] Harrington was clearly in the groove at this point, and after stating American people living in poverty would not see the benefit of education, he went on to write:

On another level, the emotions of the other America are even more profoundly disturbed. Here it is not a lack of aspiration and of hope; it is a matter of personal chaos. The drunkenness, the unstable marriages, the violence of the other America are not simply facts about individuals. They are the description of an entire group in the society who react this way because of the conditions under which they live.[39]

Harrington's investigations in the early 1960s occurred during the same period that poverty was 'rediscovered' in the UK. Following the expansion of the welfare state and the relatively stable economic period of the years following the Second World War, poverty became a 'forgotten problem' in the UK in the 1950s, and most people believed it had all but been eradicated.[40] This view was challenged by a small number of academics including, most notably, the social policy researcher Peter Townsend, who argued that poverty was not a static concept that related to a person's basic needs – such as food, shelter and clothing – being unmet. Townsend, who became arguably the most influential poverty researcher in the world, instead suggested that poverty should be understood as a relative concept, and one that was dynamic and dependent on individuals' or families' personal circumstances as well as of those around them.[41]

Once again, as with Booth's work, one might hope that the intervening period would have witnessed an improvement in the way that people experiencing poverty are discussed and represented. There is widespread political acceptance on both sides of the Atlantic that poverty is an issue and, in the UK at least, there is over a century's worth of social scientific research which highlights the primarily structural causes of poverty.[42] A large amount of this research draws on the testimonies of people experiencing poverty and those that are unable to find good, secure long-term work.[43] Very little, if any, of this academic research has found any evidence of an 'underclass' or a 'submerged tenth' among us who exhibit different norms or behaviours to 'the rest of us'.[44] And yet many politicians and their compliant 'lackey intellectuals'[45] in certain think tanks and broadsheet newspapers continue to suggest that poor families are a different breed to the 'hardworking' majority.

BROKEN BRITAIN

When Tony Blair made the historic pledge to end child poverty 'forever' in 1999,[46] the then chancellor of the exchequer Gordon Brown called the issue 'a scar on the soul of the nation', suggesting it was something that we all had to bear responsibility for.[47] In the later years of the Labour governments, however, efforts to tackle poverty and social exclusion became increasingly focused on small numbers of 'hard to reach' or 'problem' families, with the implication being that earlier policies had largely been successful in tackling these issues.[48] Whilst Labour, in government, were keen to play down the scale of social problems, the Conservatives, in opposition, were attempting to argue that the nation was at breaking point because of a wide range of social ills. Iain Duncan Smith, a one-time leader of the Conservative Party, 'discovered' his passion for social justice in 2006 following earlier trips to Easterhouse in Glasgow, where he saw first-hand the levels of deprivation that many families experienced on a daily basis. Smith established the think tank the Centre for Social Justice (CSJ) when he lost the leadership of the Conservatives, and the narrative of a 'broken society' was established.

The CSJ published two reports – 'Breakdown Britain'[49] and 'Breakthrough Britain'[50] – whilst servicing the Conservative Party social justice policy group, one of six such groups established by David Cameron in the early stages of his leadership. These reports focused on the issue of 'social breakdown', which often merged with 'family breakdown' and 'broken and dysfunctional homes'. Five behavioural 'pathways to poverty' were announced – family breakdown, educational failure, worklessness and economic dependency, addiction, and indebtedness –

and in 'Breakthrough Britain', Duncan Smith articulated where, in his view, these 'pathways' ultimately led:

> As the fabric of society crumbles at the margins what has been left behind is an underclass, where life is characterised by dependency, addiction, debt and family breakdown. This is an underclass in which a child born into poverty today is more likely to remain in poverty than at any time since the late 1960s. Bob Holman summed it up when he said that the inner city wasn't a place; it was a state of mind – there is a mentality of entrapment, where aspiration and hope are for other people, who live in another place.[51]

Cameron picked up on the 'broken society' theme, using it frequently in speeches and interviews, and referring to a by-election in Glasgow East as 'the broken society by-election'.[52] Cameron's friends at the *Sun* newspaper, Rebekah Brooks and Rupert Murdoch, helpfully (for him) ran a 'Broken Britain' campaign in 2008,[53] and in an interview with the newspaper, he said, 'I applaud The Sun's Broken Britain campaign. You are absolutely on to the right thing'.[54]

While the Conservatives were in opposition, the 'broken society' narrative remained largely focused on the alleged behavioural failings or shortcomings of individuals or families, and the problem was portrayed, as we have seen, as a national issue. Upon entering office, and the installation of Duncan Smith as secretary of state for work and pensions, this pathologisation of people living in poverty became increasingly focused on 'polluted spaces': putatively problematic towns and neigh-bourhoods that had 'been left behind', variously referred to as 'welfare ghettos', 'men deserts' and 'dumping grounds'.[55] The CSJ, working with 'grassroots' organisations in these areas, made great play of their willingness to travel to marginalised locations in order to 'see with their own eyes' the problems that exist there:

> We travelled over 50,000 miles, conducted nearly 150 evidence hearings, visited almost 1,000 poverty-fighting charities and polled 6,000 members of the public to discover first-hand what is fuelling poverty.[56]

Thus, and despite the work of researchers such as Seebohm Rowntree and Charles Booth, who conducted surveys of poverty in Victorian and

Edwardian times, and Peter Townsend, who 'rediscovered' poverty in the UK in the 1950s, individuals involved with the CSJ have attempted to present themselves as a group of pioneering social explorers, mapping out uncharted territory, just as others did before them. Whilst members of the CSJ would no doubt like to place themselves alongside renowned research figures, their approach to their subjects suggest that they should be more closely aligned with the journalist slummers who entered poor neighbourhoods in search of salacious details about the people that lived there.

The response of three influential and powerful individuals associated with the CSJ to the 'poverty porn' television programme *Benefits Street* is instructive in understanding this 'pioneering' exploration of Britain's poorer neighbourhoods.[57] *Benefits Street* was a Channel 4 'documentary' programme that promised to reveal the reality of living on benefits. It was largely derided as mocking the people who took part in the programme, and numerous charities and other organisations working with disadvantaged groups called for it to be taken off air. The three members of the CSJ, however, thought the programme offered the middle classes an insight into life in poor areas and used spatialised imagery to portray these neighbourhoods as different 'worlds' or 'countries', no doubt where people who were different from, and no doubt less developed than, 'the rest of us' resided.

Fraser Nelson, a member of the CSJ's advisory board, used his day job as columnist for the *Daily Telegraph* and editor of the *Spectator* to argue that:

> No scandal has been more successfully covered up than the appalling truth about what happens to Britain's poorest people. We have, as a country, grown used to pretending they don't exist; we shovel them off to edge-of-town housing estates and pay them to stay there in economic exile. We give them welfare for the foreseeable future, and wish them luck in their drug-addled welfare ghettos. This is our country's dirty little secret.[58]

Nelson was only warming up with this opening paragraph. He went on to suggest that the reason *Benefits Street* had been so popular with viewers was because 'it offers a glimpse into what has now become, to most British people, another country'.[59] Nelson was also keen to point out that such areas existed not just in Birmingham, the location for the first series of *Benefits Street*, for there were numerous areas that could be considered as being more deprived. He namechecked wards in Liverpool, Manchester and Newcastle before stating, in relation to Calton in Glasgow, that he 'discovered, male life expectancy at birth is just 54 – on a par with Uganda'.[60] Nelson, reflecting on the criticism that *Benefits Street* attracted from 'the left', then mused: 'Make a documentary about poverty in Uganda and you could win an award. Look at problems in Britain and you're reported for thought crime'.[61]

Iain Duncan Smith himself then got in on the act, arguing that whilst 'the middle class majority were aware of the problems in poor communities, they remained largely unaware of the true nature of life on some of our estates'.[62] The problem, according to Duncan Smith, was 'a benefits system that traps people, leaving them in a twilight world', and that 'for too long we let these problems be ghettoised as though they were a different country'.[63]

Christian Guy, at the time director of the CSJ, then wrote a piece for the *Huffington Post* less than a week later, where he argued that '[r]ecent work by the Centre for Social Justice has revealed shocking levels of deprivation in pockets all over the UK'.[64] This 'shocking' level of deprivation had, according to Guy, not reached the public conscience because '[t]hey [the poor] have been housed on the margins of society; kept quiet in a second Britain' – a statement echoing Harrington's argument of a 'second America' from 50 years earlier.[65]

Similar comments have been heard in Parliament, where Baroness Rosalind Grender, a Liberal Democrat peer, claimed that families involved in the government's Troubled Families Programme were living 'in a world that is almost unrecognisable'.[66] This statement was made despite the wealth of evidence highlighting that the vast majority of officially labelled 'troubled families' are not cut off from the rest of society in any way, shape or form.[67] Grender, however, appears to be slightly out of touch with mainstream views and norms, as she has previously suggested that being a member of the House of Lords was 'unaffordable' for ordinary people such as hairdressers and bus drivers, because the daily tax-free allowance of £300 per day left people reliant on their partner's income.[68]

Whilst these references to 'another country', a 'second Britain' and 'an unrecognisable world' of disadvantaged neighbourhoods manage to retain some semblance of discretion or restraint on the part of the authors, the same cannot be said of Rachel Johnson's description of her experience during the making of a BBC television documentary titled *Famous, Rich and Hungry*. Johnson is the sister of the former mayor of London and current foreign secretary, Boris Johnson. She was privately educated, attended Oxford University and is the former editor of *The Lady*, referred to by the *Independent* as 'arguably the world's poshest magazine'.[69]

In 2014, Rachel Johnson was invited to spend a week living on a low income to 'experience' how people living in poverty fared and how they managed to eat on this budget. She spent time with a family in East London where there was often little more than £1 per day for food. She referred to her experience as a 'poverty safari' and expressed the view that people forced to live on low incomes were 'existing, rather than living, like battery hens. Apart from the telly and the cigarettes, they are living like animals'.[70] The remarks unsurprisingly made headlines, but Johnson defended them and suggested that people should be angry, not at her but at the fact that people are forced to live in such conditions, as though it was a choice between one or the other. Johnson's 'wealthy, privileged friends' were 'almost jealous' of Johnson's 'meaningful, even enriching, experience [which] they couldn't buy',[71] demonstrating, as Sibley argued, that 'defiled people and places offer excitement'.[72] Johnson's use of the term 'poverty safari' also takes on racial undertones given the ethnic diversity of the East End of London today. One participant in a recent research project examining how residents of the predominantly white, middle-class district of East Dulwich viewed a nearby multi-ethnic area referred to it as 'deepest, darkest Peckham', whilst another spoke of it as 'another world'.[73] The *Radio Times* helpfully informed its readers that Johnson had sent 'thank you' notes and a jar of home-made jam to 'her hosts on Planet Poverty'.[74]

Johnson's position, and that of her envious friends, shares obvious similarities not only with the slumming practices of Victorian times but also with the modern-day practice of 'doing the slum' during overseas holidays. Trips to see impoverished neighbourhoods in developing countries are a growing industry and are, in fact, an experience that those with money can buy.[75] Johnson's friends, however, bemoan the fact that there is no longer a domestic practice of slumming to provide them with the 'meaningful' or 'enriching' experiences they evidently crave.

'LANDSCAPES OF STRANGERS AND SECRETS'

This chapter has focused on how people living in poverty in the UK (and also, at times, the USA) have been compared to inhabitants of other countries or as 'an exotic species' in various ways. Although most recent discourses surrounding the Otherness of people living in poverty do not make explicit links between African pygmies and 'vicious lazy louts' in the way that Booth did in the nineteenth century, the traces of this unpalatable position can still be found in the way that some contemporary 'social reformers' discuss those who are forced to live on low incomes. Government ministers, their advisors and their friends in the mainstream media have all hinted, some more subtly than others, of their contempt for the alleged behaviour of many people living in relatively close proximity to them. The specific words may have changed, but the views have not. Although they may be masked by discourses about 'social justice' or cloaked in celebrity philanthropic endeavours, attitudes towards 'the poor' remain largely unchanged in some quarters.

It is fairly obvious that 'another country' does not refer to nations such as France, Germany, Sweden, Canada, Australia or other 'developed' and 'civilised' states. The 'other country' that is referred to is one that is reputedly less developed, and more primitive, than our own 'beloved island'. Although the term 'darkest Africa' has yet to re-emerge, the symbolically potent idea of a 'poverty safari' and explicit comparisons with countries such as Uganda mean that such blunt phrases are no longer required. In this way, the Victorian perspective of 'seeing' poverty at home as being synonymous with other exotic and adventurous imperialist missions further afield lives on. Ideas about the superiority of the British middle classes show no sign of letting up. The 'twilight world' of welfare dependency that Duncan Smith refers to elicits feelings of mystery, anxiety and the unfamiliar, feelings of nervous excitement that the original social explorers must have felt in the late nineteenth century, or what middle-class travellers of today might experience whilst 'doing the slum' on foreign holidays.

Portraying people on low incomes as 'exotic Others' as opposed to 'familiar' or 'proximate' others not only helps to create further distance between 'them' and 'us', it also points to the 'root causes' and 'drivers' of poverty, in the parlance of the CSJ. People living in poverty are thus portrayed as being 'more primitive' than more affluent members of the middle classes or 'the establishment'. In this narrative, they themselves are the chief architects of their own circumstances. They have failed to see, understand or grasp the opportunities provided by a benign and caring society that has attempted to offer a hand to help people get out of the social depths. The cruel myth of a meritocracy suggests that people experiencing hardship do so because they have been unable or unwilling to extricate themselves from poverty, unlike other, more socially mobile members of the working class.

Within this exotic imagery of phantasms, of 'twilight worlds' and the like, there remains little room for 'familiar' or more 'mundane' others. The cleaner, employed on a zero-hours contract, who works in the same office block and shares the same public transport as other commuters, the retail assistants who serve members of the public in shops and cafes, or the people who provide social care for elderly parents and grandparents do not neatly fit the picture of disadvantaged members of society being 'an exotic species'. It is difficult, if not impossible, to Other these people, because, as a society, we are so dependent on them, and countless others who work in similar precarious and poorly paid occupations. The spaces occupied and traversed by these people cannot be portrayed as far off, exotic and unknown destinations because they are the same spaces that millions of people use every day. It is only through the imaginary geographies of 'twilight worlds' and 'other countries' in which our poor people allegedly live that politicians and spontaneous sociologists can successfully Other large sections of the population. These images of the 'unknown' also help to maintain their view that, by virtue of them having seen things 'with their own eyes', they are best placed to comment on social issues such as poverty and social exclusion. As Judith R. Walkowitz, a professor of history and women's studies, has observed about the gentleman *flaneurs* of the Victorian era, fact and fantasy often became entwined in their desire to 'transform the city into a landscape of strangers and secrets'.[76]

3
Tales of Two Cities

Marginal places, those towns and regions which have been 'left behind' in the modern race for progress, evoke both nostalgia and fascination. Their marginal status may come from out-of-the-way geographical locations, being the site of illicit or disdained social activities, or being the Other to some great cultural centre ... They all carry the image, and stigma, of their marginality which becomes indistinguishable from any basic empirical identity they might once have had.

Rob Shields, 1991.[1]

Poverty is overwhelmingly portrayed as an urban problem, with rural poverty receiving relatively little attention from researchers, policymakers or the media. Some towns and cities, such as Middlesbrough and Grimsby in England, Dundee in Scotland and Detroit in the United States, come to be synonymous with poverty and 'urban decay', often as a result of deindustrialisation and changing economic forces that have stripped them of jobs. In response to these issues, some places have attempted to transform themselves into 'creative cities', in a concerted effort to persuade members of the creative class to relocate to them, or at least visit them for a city break, and help new knowledge-based and cultural economies to grow out of the abandoned and derelict warehouses and factories. Glasgow in Scotland and Manchester and Newcastle in England are examples of cities with industrial heritages that now attempt to present themselves as cultural destinations.

This chapter examines tales of these two types of cities. The first part of the chapter explores the ways in which struggling, deindustrialised cities and regions are portrayed as anachronistic spaces, 'existing at the same point in time, yet somehow not belonging in the time of the present'.[2] Some of these cities come to be known primarily for their marginalisation and lack of 'progress'. The American city of Detroit and the north-east of England are used as examples of the nostalgia and fascination of spaces that are sometimes depicted as 'dead' or 'dying'. The second half of the chapter examines what might be called the imagined geographies of affluence, or culture: attempts by cities to portray themselves as vibrant, cultural locales, which often include the exclusion of people living on low incomes and other marginalised populations. Developments such as anti-homelessness spikes, 'poor doors' and temporary fences, which see the urban environment redesigned to exclude or prevent the movement of poorer populations and reimagined as 'purified spaces', are interrogated here. The chapter concludes with a discussion of the aestheticising of urban poverty in some locations and the masking or denial of it in others.

DETROITISM

In a newspaper article promoting his film *Requiem for Detroit?*, the film-maker Julien Temple set out an apocalyptic vision of the city:

> [I]t's hard to believe what we're seeing. The vast, rusting hulks of abandoned car plants, (some of the largest structures ever built and far too expensive to pull down), beached amid a shining sea of grass. The blackened corpses of hundreds of burned-out houses, pulled back to earth by the green tentacles of nature. Only the drunken rows of telegraph poles marching away across acres of wildflowers and prairie give any clue as to where teeming city streets might once have been.
>
> Approaching the derelict shell of downtown Detroit, we see full-grown trees sprouting from the tops of deserted skyscrapers. In their shadows, the glazed eyes of the street zombies slide into view, stumbling in front of the car.[3]

Temple's 'mad-dog enthusiasm' for filming abandoned parts of the city – 'everywhere demands to be filmed', he claims – provides an exemplar of the 'ruin porn' that Detroit has been subjected to in recent years, what John Patrick Leary, an American professor of English, has called 'the exuberant connoisseurship of dereliction'.[4] Ruin porn invariably involves photographers and other members of the creative class getting their kicks by turning the remnants of the automotive and other industries in Detroit into opportunities for artistic and aesthetic self-actualisation. Glossy books called *Detroit Disassembled* and *The Ruins of Detroit* have been published,[5] the phenomenon has attracted lots of online attention and photographers from a wide range of American publications have descended on the city in recent years, keen to photograph the 'Mecca of the urban ruins'.[6]

The Pontiac Silverdome, the former home of the American football team the Detroit Lions and the basketball team the Detroit Pistons, is one of the ruins that has set young, creative urban types, and the corporations they are aligned with, salivating. Opened in 1975, the Silverdome was, at the time, the largest stadium in the National Football League and the first ever football World Cup indoor venue. The Lions left the Silverdome in 2002 to play at the newly opened Ford Field and, since that date, the stadium has struggled to survive, closing and reopening at one point, and being scheduled for demolition in early 2016. Red Bull, the energy drinks company that sponsors a wide range of urban and extreme sports events, shot and produced a promotional video in the ruined stadium in 2015.[7] It was released on YouTube and features the Detroit-born BMX rider Tyler Fernengel. The stylish three-and-a-half-minute video shows Fernengel riding through the empty, derelict and dilapidated stadium, and ends with him pedalling from an executive suite, through a window missing its glass, onto a ramp set up over broken plastic seating and onto a jump in the centre of the playing field, across the ripped up and largely absent artificial turf. Red Bull have also shot scenes for a skiing film in Detroit, featuring skiers jumping off and over various derelict buildings in 'the concrete jungle that is Detroit' to a backdrop of police sirens, with the sounds emphasising the 'danger' they are facing in pursuing their art.[8]

The photographer Jonny Joo also negotiated access to the Silverdome in 2013 and 2014 and took a series of photographs as part of his 'architectural afterlife' collection.[9] In a blog post about his visits, Joo sets out a short history of the stadium before describing a visit that included entering a former dining hall that was being 'reclaimed' by nature:

> From the windows, the entire stadium grounds outside are visible, and where some windows have been shattered, nature begins to welcome itself in for a drink. At the base of many of these glass panels, where water damage has invited its way into the carpet, a brand new, bright green carpet of moss has begun a natural installation. Where condiments sit atop shelves, a jungle of green begins to consume them from the daily sun welcomed in through the massive glass panes. As you wander past tables, the entire room smells of water damage, while

the stadium view remains as beautiful as ever. It's like looking off into the apocalypse.[10]

Ruin porn has been criticised as being a form of art that is 'based purely on aesthetics and is almost always devoid of people'.[11] The population of Detroit, which still numbers well in excess of half a million, is written out of the picture, with the return of 'nature' in unexpected urban settings symbolising the absence, or withering, of civilisation.[12] Structures are 'beached amid a shining sea of grass' or 'pulled back to earth by the green tentacles of nature', and 'jungles of green' begin to reclaim what was once a site of civilisation. Sibley notes in *Geographies of Exclusion* how nature has a long historical association with the Other and how indigenous populations are Othered by virtue of their presumed proximity to nature: 'If they are part of nature, they are less than human'.[13]

In Victorian London, the middle classes would visit poor neighbourhoods to gawk at the people living there; in Detroit, they now go slumming to 'admire' the derelict buildings and 'learn' of the city's recent history – an exemplar of the nostalgia and fascination for 'marginal places' described above by Shields.[14] In concluding his blog post about his exploration of the 'apocalypse stadium', Joo writes that when he was in the middle of the pitch, 'I truly felt that I was lost in a reality shift, thrown into a life after people'; when describing his feelings whilst on the stadium's roof, he writes: 'though I knew there was life outside these walls, the world felt quiet and empty. I was on top of the empty world'.[15]

In a gripping essay on 'Detroitism', Leary argues that, 'So much ruin photography and ruin film aestheticizes poverty without inquiring of its origins, dramatizes spaces but never seeks out the people that inhabit and transform them'.[16] Such a focus on empty spaces and buildings suggests that there is no life to be found there, that these sites belong to another time. The exclusion of people ensures that narratives of any kind, never mind those that might present a different picture to the ones that 'ruin photographers' present, do not accompany the images. The day-to-day life of the people living in such areas remains an unwelcome and no doubt jarring distraction from the 'elegance', 'simplicity' and 'silence' of much ruin porn. The photographs thus stand alone, capturing a moment in time, but one that is also presented as being atemporal, with little or no historical context. As Leary notes, however:

no photograph can adequately identify the origins for Detroit's contemporary ruination; all it can represent is the spectacular wreckage left behind in the present, after decades of deindustrialization, housing discrimination, suburbanization, drug violence, municipal corruption and incompetence, highway construction, and other forms of urban renewal have taken their terrible tolls.[17]

Thus the focus on the tangible local dereliction that remains serves to obscure or deflect attention away from the things that have been taken away and, even more so, from the ways in which they were taken away. Political decisions and projects are not easily photographed; images of government policy documents are not as aesthetically interesting or 'exciting' as images of desolate, faux-apocalyptic urban environments; the absence of jobs is implied by many of the photographs, but it is of secondary import to the primary goal of aestheticising abandonment.

Leary identifies two groups within the ruin porn genre: those who lament Detroit's decline and those who see opportunity in it. The film-maker Julien Temple undoubtedly falls into the latter, and his 'mad dog enthusiasm' for Detroit does not end with his admiration for the photographic opportunities the city presents. He is also wildly optimistic about its future:

Although the city is still haemorrhaging population, young people from all over the country are also flooding into Detroit – artists, musicians and social pioneers, all keen to make use of the abandoned urban spaces and create new ways of living together.

With the breakdown of 20th-century civilisation, many Detroiters have discovered an exhilarating sense of starting over, building together a new cross-racial community sense of doing things, discarding the bankrupt rules of the past and taking direct control of their own lives. Still at the forefront of the American Dream, Detroit is fast becoming the first 'post-American' city. And amid the ruins of the Motor City it is possible to find a first pioneer's map to the post-industrial future that awaits us all. So perhaps Detroit can avoid the fate of the lost cities of the Maya and rise again like the phoenix that sits, appropriately, on its municipal crest.[18]

'New blood' from the 'creative class' is thus required to help drag the existing, stale, 'zombiefied' population out of its current stupor and prevent the city going the way of the 'lost cities of the Maya'.

Although it has got some way to go before becoming associated with ruin porn in the same way as Detroit, the north-east of England is often portrayed in similar ways, and has been referred to as 'Britain's Detroit', the 'next Detroit' and as part of the British 'rustbelt' in recent years. There are a number of parallels and overlaps between the way the two are portrayed, especially in relation to the consequences of deindustrialisation, although these are not always entirely consistent.

THE BRITISH DETROIT

The north-east of England, far away from London, sharing a border with Scotland, is one of the poorest parts of the country. This region was, like Detroit, built on industry. Whilst Detroit acts as a metonym for both the automotive industry in America and the subsequent decline of that field, the north-east of England is synonymous with the rise and fall of heavy industries such as coal mining, shipbuilding and steel manufacture. In the nineteenth century, Middlesbrough was the fastest growing town in England, 'mushrooming from a rural hamlet with a population of 40 people in 1820 to a bustling industrial town with a population of over 90,000 residents' by the end of the century.[19] The Teesside skyline at night, a mixture of vast industrial architecture, bright lights, smoke and flames, served, in part, as the inspiration for the dystopian cityscape featured in Ridley Scott's classic sci-fi film *Blade Runner*.[20] The steel produced on Teesside helped to build iconic structures of the twentieth century such as the Tyne Bridge, Sydney Harbour Bridge and Auckland Harbour Bridge, but by 2016 the coke ovens in Redcar had been extinguished and there appeared little prospect of steelmaking continuing in the region in the near future.

In recent years, journalists have visited the north-east to 'understand' the effects of deindustrialisation and austerity on the region. In 2011, Landon Thomas Jr., a journalist with the *New York Times*, wrote that austerity measures and cuts to public services would 'be most keenly felt across the iron and steel belt of this country's depressed northeast, in places like Middlesbrough, which in many ways is a British version of Detroit'.[21] Michael Goldfarb, an American journalist and author, warned in 2013 that 'income inequality is climbing and threatens to return places like Middlesbrough to a Dickensian age of "haves" and "have-nots".'[22]

The depiction of the north-east as being isolated and 'remote' and 'more like an island than a region', as an article in the *Guardian* by Andy Beckett in 2014 suggested, is perhaps slightly unfair.[23] Newcastle, at the centre of the region, has an international airport and can be reached by train from London in three hours and from Edinburgh in two hours. Over 2.5 million people live in the region, but as Rob Shields argued in *Places on the Margin*, it is cultural and social isolation, rather than any physical isolation, that is implied by the spatial reference.[24]

In Beckett's article, the island simile, advanced by Harry Pearson in his book *The Far Corner*,[25] is augmented by other quotes which suggest that the north-east is full of people who have 'just been cut loose', a place where people now constitute an inferior population that is lagging behind.[26] 'New blood' is once again proposed as the answer, with the Labour Party MP for Newcastle Central bemoaning the fact that the region has not 'got enough skills and entrepreneurs', whilst one entrepreneur interviewed for the piece stated that 'persuading clever people from the south to come here is quite hard'.[27] People living in the north-east are thus presented, with the help of spatial symbolism, as Others: different and, more specifically, 'dull and backward', albeit in slightly more euphemistic language than the Women's Group on Public Welfare managed in their report *Our Towns* in 1943.[28]

The problems experienced *by* the region are presented as being problems *of* the region. Although Beckett references the deindustrialisation that the region has experienced, the article still manages to convey the impression that the north-east has not played the hand it has been dealt particularly well. He bemoans the fact that an art gallery in Middlesbrough does not attract more visitors when it opens late once a week and, strangely, appears offended by 'cheap cafes [that] offer soup of the day for a pound'.[29] What the north-east lacks, obviously, just like Detroit, is culture and a burgeoning creative and entrepreneurial class who could engender an 'exhilarating sense of starting over' amidst the desolation, perhaps whilst 'spotting the potential' of disadvantaged neighbourhoods and selling bowls of cereal for £3 a go, as 'entrepreneurs' in Brixton have done. If only, the argument goes, working-class places had more middle-class facilities and eateries, people's experience of poverty would be so much better.

Whilst some commentators see a future for towns, cities and regions that are struggling, others see little point in attempting to 'regenerate' towns such as Middlesbrough and Sunderland. Another influential right-wing think tank, Policy Exchange, produced a report in 2007 that argued, 'It is time to stop pretending that there is a bright future for Sunderland and ask ourselves instead what we need to do to offer people in Sunderland better prospects'.[30] Yet again, the problems experienced by these towns are presented as problems of those towns. The authors argue that, 'just as we can't buck the market, so we can't buck economic geography either',[31] presenting the concentration of wealth in the UK in the south-east as an unstoppable force of nature. Their answer is to embrace this irresistible force by encouraging significant numbers of people to move to London and the south-east and liberalising land use in the same areas. The south-east and the capital are 'economic powerhouses that can grow and create high-skilled, high-wage service-sector hubs.[32]

Bourdieu suggested that people like the authors of this report were 'young technocrats who often know almost nothing about the daily lives of their fellow citizens and have no occasion to be reminded of their ignorance'.[33] Elsewhere, he referred to them as 'half-wise economists', people who, 'obsessed by the question of financial equilibrium',

> fail, of course, to take account of the real costs, in the short and more especially the long term, of the material and psychological wretchedness which is the only certain outcome of their economically legitimate Realpolitik: delinquency, crime, alcoholism, road accidents, etc.[34]

Reports produced in London for a Westminster audience, then, rarely examine what leaving behind family, friends and systems of social support might mean for people forced to leave or for people forced to remain. The number of low-paid, insecure, poor-quality jobs that are required to keep the 'creative classes' in the lifestyle to which they have become accustomed rarely merits a mention or even an acknowledgement. More restaurants mean more waiting jobs, more kitchen porter jobs. Nor do similar reports highlight the fact that such jobs need not be poorly paid, or insecure or of poor quality. There is nothing 'natural' about in-work poverty, and the 'half-wise economists' who produce such reports should 'stop pretending' that there is nothing that we can do to 'buck the market'.

THE NEW 'NO-GO AREAS'

People living on low incomes or those in search of work are expected to be flexible and mobile, willing to uproot or leave their families at a moment's notice in search of a better life in more prosperous, entrepreneurial and 'vibrant' cities. But there are precious few urban policies which demonstrate an inclusive or welcoming approach towards marginalised groups. There are, in contrast, numerous examples of 'defensive' or 'hostile' responses that appear designed to keep people living in or at risk of poverty, out of sight and out of mind.

'Defensive architecture', which was previously known as 'hostile architecture', refers to physical design features which prevent objects being used for anything other than their intended purpose. Perhaps the best known examples are 'anti-homelessness spikes' which can now be found on flat sheltered spaces, often immediately outside shops, offices and apartments in many cities across the world, to prevent homeless people from sitting or sleeping there.[35] The 'Camden bench', an ugly sloping concrete bench which ensures that it cannot be used for sleeping on and reduces opportunities for littering, has also achieved infamy following its installation in 'feature sites' across the London borough.[36] Whilst defensive architecture has been used to prevent skateboarding and general loitering, it is its use to prevent homeless people from sleeping in particular places which has led some critics to argue that the practice equates to attempts to 'design the homeless out of cities' and that it merely represents 'a cheap alternative to investing in more appropriate and humane responses to homelessness, such as shelters, social services and police action'.[37]

In an example of temporary defensive architecture, an eight-foot-high metal fence complete with CCTV cameras was installed in Glasgow for the duration of the Commonwealth Games in 2014.[38] The fence 'protected' the athlete's village but it also meant that residents of a nearby housing estate were almost 'barricaded' into their neighbourhood, with severe disruption to their daily lives caused by the installation. This development, it is worth noting, came after the scrapping of a plan to blow up the iconic Red Road Flats in Glasgow in preparation for the games – a marketing stunt of remarkably bad taste, which drew an overwhelmingly negative response from almost everyone who heard about it.[39]

The Red Road Flats and the fence surrounding the athlete's village highlight the symbolic work that changes to physical spaces can do. The 'old' Glasgow, in the form of the flats, had to make way for the 'new' Glasgow or, where this wasn't possible, 'old' Glasgow residents had to be kept out of the way and 'excluded' as much as possible, especially where the athletes were concerned. Residents in the poorer East End of the city, which was most affected by these changes, recognised that 'had this been the [more prosperous] west end, such things would have never been allowed to happen'.⁴⁰ These efforts are merely the latest in a long line of attempt to re-make the city and 'wrap it in tinsel'. As one commentator noted, writing during the early 1990s:

> Glasgow is in the process of acquiring a new identity: Its legends are being unpicked and remade: The noisy Clyde of yesteryear became the quiet lachrymose Clyde of the recession, which in turn is being transformed by the image-makers into the cultured Clyde of 1990. But this semiotic package of half-truths which wraps Glasgow in tinsel is a myth of Sorelian proportions which – while providing an afflatus for the busy, local bourgeoisie – is little more than a slap in the face for those citizens who have to live in the 'dreadful enclosures' which scar the city.⁴¹

Another architectural 'innovation' that has drawn widespread anger and disbelief is the advent of so-called 'poor doors' in London, having arrived from New York.⁴² 'Poor doors' are separate entrances to apartment blocks, installed specifically for people living in 'affordable' units within the blocks and helping to ensure that the more opulent lobbies accessed by 'front doors' remain as 'purified spaces', free from polluting populations. Perhaps the best known example is the development at One Commercial Street in London, where privately owned apartments are marketed to city traders and accessed through a 'luxury lobby'.⁴³ By contrast, the affordable housing units at the same address are accessed through a side door down an alley. Other spaces associated with residency in such blocks such as lifts, bicycle storage spaces, rubbish disposal facilities and postal deliveries are also being segregated so that the people sharing the same address, but occupying entirely different social spaces, are not required to ever share the same physical space. Different floors within blocks of apartments are often set aside for social housing tenants to ensure that all private communal areas, as far as possible, remain 'purified'.

One Commercial Street is owned by Hondo Enterprises, which is run by Taylor McWilliams, a Texan associate of Prince Harry who also goes by the name of DJ Junctional Funky. In an interview with the UK edition of the style magazine *Elle*, he revealed how he liked to spend his weekends in London, listing a host of exclusive and expensive cafés, restaurants, bars and clubs, including an organic sprout juicer in Battersea where he recommended one of their 'tailored juice cleanses' after 'a few too many vodka sodas' on a Saturday night.[44] The article also revealed that he was planning to develop a new hotel in Shoreditch, complete with spa, restaurant and rooftop pool and bar. The contrast between the 'jet-set lifestyle' of the international playboy developer and the people living in one of his properties, but denied access to certain spaces by his company's use of 'poor doors' and deemed 'off-limits' to them, could hardly be greater.

There has also been an increase in what might be called a 'defensive' or 'hostile' politics of space in recent years, both locally and nationally: the Anti-Social Behaviour, Crime and Policing Act 2014 gave police powers to bar or disperse individuals from public spaces if they were causing 'harassment, alarm or distress' to others in the same space;[45] Hackney Council attempted to make rough sleeping a criminal offence within a designated area;[46] Newcastle City Council inaugurated a 'No Need to Beg' campaign, which preferred to highlight the effect that begging had on local businesses, rather than the effect that homelessness had on individuals.[47] A briefing by the campaigning organisation the Manifesto Club has highlighted how these new powers are being used in a 'pre-emptive and unjust manner' to exclude homeless people and other marginalised groups from social occasions such as the switching on of Christmas lights, Halloween and bonfire night and fireworks displays.[48] The report also noted that dispersal zones were created in anticipation of the South Staffordshire Victorian fair and the Long Eaton Chestnut Fair, which are not known to be hotbeds of debauchery and depravity.[49] The long-term conflation of poverty with nuisance and criminality shows no signs of abating, especially in urban areas.

PURIFIED SPACES AND A 'FILTHY CIVILISATION'

In the heavily aestheticised ruin porn of Detroit, images of local people moving mundanely through the streetscapes or around the empty buildings on foot rarely feature, but images often include people traversing the city, in exciting ways, such as on skis or BMX bikes. These culturally rich interlopers are presented as mobile, both within and around the derelict buildings, but also in terms of where they work and the different cities, nations and continents they travel to. The only everyday local people left are referred to as 'street zombies', the residuum that remains in an apocalyptic landscape where everyone that can has moved out and where nature is reclaiming what 'civilisation' has left behind.

In the UK, the north-east of England has been compared with Detroit and portrayed as a former industrial heartland whose best days are behind it and apparently in danger of 'falling behind' the rest of the country. The residents do not access cultural opportunities and therefore the region's future depends on 'clever people' and 'entrepreneurs' moving in from elsewhere. Thus, both Detroit and the north-east of England are portrayed as anachronistic spaces, not fully belonging in the present and failing to make the 'progress' that the rest of the country is allegedly making. These cities reputedly lack the culture, skills and knowledge that, it seems, can only be provided by importing them from elsewhere. The 'problems' associated with these places are portrayed as 'problems' of the places and, indeed, of the people that reside there.

In more affluent, 'vibrant' cities – the 'great cultural centres' that Shields mentions[50] – steps are often taken to exclude people in economically marginalised positions from certain areas, or to limit their movement within them. Working-class people are not allowed to use the same entrance as other, more affluent residents, if they are guilty of living in 'affordable' accommodation. Whole estates are 'barricaded in' during cultural events. Being homeless is increasingly being viewed as a 'nuisance' to businesses and consumers, which requires the 'offender' to be removed or excluded from spaces of consumption, rather than being treated as a social issue that demands a humane response. Cities such as London and Glasgow evidently do not want their global imagery as 'purified spaces' of cultural consumption spoiled by the realities of urban inequality and deprivation. Signs of inequality and abject poverty ruin the view from a rooftop bar.

The focus on the remnants of disinvestment and deindustrialisation in locations like Detroit and Middlesbrough often crowds out any discussion about the processes that led to such dereliction and hardship. Similarly, discussions of the vibrancy and cultural opportunities to be found in cities that are in the process of being 'remade', such as Glasgow and London, give little room for consideration of the poverty and inequality that remain, often just around the corner.

The English textile designer, novelist and socialist William Morris argued that Victorian smoke stacks and factory chimneys that polluted the atmosphere were, along with slum neighbourhoods, signs of 'the incredible filth, disorder, and degradation of modern civilization'.[51] Elsewhere, in his essay 'How I Became a Socialist', Morris argued that the inequality that was present in Victorian times and the pursuit of wealth at all cost was evidence of the 'filth of civilization'.[52] According to Morris, the 'contempt of simple pleasures' and growing levels of poverty and misery were tolerated if economic growth could be sustained and if 'progress' was being made. Today, with Victorian levels of inequality predicted to return, when deliberate and coordinated disinvestment and lack of good work leads to poverty, and when our authorities attempt to realise the 'supreme fiction' of 'purified spaces', ensuring that poor people do not 'spoil' the view in vibrant cities, it is hard to mount any kind of argument that civilisation in the twenty-first century is any less filthy.

The reality of Detroit cannot be adequately explained through the photographic exploration of its ruins and derelict buildings, devoid of any accompanying narrative, nor can north-east England's current economic marginalisation be explicated by a couple of short trips to the region, or afternoon tea with the local mayor.[53] Attempts to understand the 'regeneration' and remaking of city centres in the UK, and their attempts to attract visitors need also to include consideration of extensive efforts to exclude or erase other groups of people from the same spaces. Many poor people are not welcome in parts of large cities where aestheticism and vibrancy is prioritised over inclusivity and social justice. These political processes and economic forces, which do so much to shape places, remain undiscussed and marginalised. The camera eye of ruin porn may not lie, but it certainly does not tell the whole truth.

4

Neighbourhood Effects or Westminster Effects?

> Certain milieu gather reputations for moral inferiority, squalor, violence, and social pathology, and consequently they objectify the fantasy of the dreadful enclosure ... According to the stereotype, housing projects are loci in which sick and dangerous people drift together in a kind of behavioural sink, producing urban capsules of pathology so highly concentrated that the ordinary resources of the body social cannot control them.
>
> E.V. Walters, 1977.[1]

Poor neighbourhoods and disadvantaged districts of cities – the 'dreadful enclosures' and 'phantasms' of urban myths – have long held a particular fascination for people from more privileged backgrounds. We have already discussed the amusement many members of the Victorian middle classes experienced via their slumming activities and noted that Friedrich Engels spent time living in Manchester in the 1840s. Since then, social researchers on both sides of the Atlantic have wanted to find out more about life in the slums and ghettos of the inner cities. Some of the first pieces of poverty-related academic research were carried out by researchers such as Charles Booth, Seebohm Rowntree and Arthur Bowley, who visited poor neighbourhoods, enquiring about the conditions in which people lived.[2] Since then, numerous influential studies, using various methodologies, have been carried out in disadvantaged neighbourhoods in cities across the world.

Politicians have also demonstrated their concern about poor neighbourhoods by visiting them. The historian Seth Koven notes that when William Beveridge, largely regarded as the 'father' of the British welfare state, first arrived at Toynbee Hall, one of the university settlements in the East End of London, 'he felt like "an American tourist doing Whitechapel in two days"'.[3] In the United States in the spring of 1964, the then president, Lyndon Johnson, embarked on a series of 'poverty tours' as part of America's 'all-out war on human poverty and unemployment'. The tours were designed to highlight just how seriously the Johnson administration was taking the issue of poverty. Flying to different impoverished towns in the presidential airplane Air Force One, and preceded by secret service officers and state troopers, Johnson was photographed visiting various families and speaking with them on their porches. Stops included towns in Appalachia, a largely white area that featured heavily in Michael Harrington's book, *The Other America*.[4] In one report of the president's visit to a farming family in North Carolina, William Marlow, the father of the family, stated that: 'After we shook hands, he [President Johnson] was just like a neighbour. He was right down to earth. And his daughter [Lynda] was just like any fine farm or city girl I've ever seen'.[5]

This chapter, however, focuses on three interventions in or about disadvantaged neighbourhoods by politicians in the UK in recent times. Firstly, I look at the comments of the former prime minister David Cameron in January 2016 about 'sink estates', leading on to a discussion about the concepts 'neighbourhood effects' and 'territorial stigmatisation'. The attention then turns to another former prime minister, Tony Blair, who gave his first speech as leader of the government in 1997 on the Aylesbury Estate in London, a disadvantaged post-war housing estate, where he claimed 'the biggest employer is the drugs industry'. The role of Easterhouse, a poor district of Glasgow, in helping Iain Duncan Smith, a former leader of the Conservative Party, to discover his passion for social justice, via numerous visits to the area, is then discussed. The chapter concludes with an argument that what might be called 'Westminster effects', both symbolic and material, *on* these neighbourhoods are arguably stronger than any putative effects emanating *from* them.

'GIFTS TO CRIMINALS'

In January 2016, whilst he was still prime minister, David Cameron launched an initiative to rid Britain of its 'sink estates' as part of his attempt to 'wage an all-out assault on poverty and disadvantage'.[6] Writing prior to making a speech on 'life chances', he told of his desire to set out a plan that would 'really get to grips with the deep social problems – the blocked opportunity, poor parenting, addiction and mental health problems'. Cameron went on to state:

There's one issue that brings together many of these social problems – and for me, epitomises both the scale of the challenge we face and the nature of state failure over decades. It's our housing estates. Some of them, especially those built just after the war, are actually entrenching poverty in Britain – isolating and entrapping many of our families and communities.

Cameron wrote that 'dark alleyways are a gift to criminals and drug dealers', and highlighted how three-quarters of people convicted of rioting in 2011 lived on post-war estates, stating 'That's not a coincidence'. He went on to argue that the estates he was talking about were 'cut off, self-governing and divorced from the mainstream', and he highlighted how a plethora of regeneration and renewal initiatives had failed to tackle the poverty and deprivation associated with many of them. His proposed answer, which garnered lots of media attention, was, in many cases, to 'tear them down' and start again.

An advisory panel would draw up a list of 'postwar estates across the country that are ripe for redevelopment'. Almost inevitably, there was a key role for the private sector to play in this project, and Cameron suggested that 'regeneration will work best where land values are high' because the sale of private homes would then help to fund the regeneration for the rest of the estate. State funding and involvement was limited to a symbolic contribution of £140 million to help 'pump-prime the planning process' and subsidise early construction costs, 'sweeping away' the 'planning blockages' and reducing 'political and reputational risk' for the key decision makers and investors in any regeneration projects.

Cameron's announcement was met with immediate criticism. The £140 million announced by Cameron to support his scheme was revealed a month later to be a loan 'to be used as a springboard for partnership and joint venture arrangements'.[7] Meanwhile, one architect argued that it heralded 'a new era of blaming buildings – rather than government welfare policy – for the socio-economic challenges facing many impoverished communities', and 'conflated the causes of poverty with the layout of a communal stairwell'.[8] Lynsey Hanley argued that Cameron's position attempted to turn cause and effect on their heads, and 'flaunts a refusal to look at the complex situations of marginalised people, not least why some people are cast, through policy and perception, to the margins in the first place'.[9]

Cameron's assertion that it was postwar 'housing estates' that represented the 'one issue' that linked so many social problems not only demonstrates the territorial stigmatisation suffered by certain impoverished locales, but it also provides an exemplar of the neighbourhood effects thesis, which argues that where you live affects your life chances.

Scholarship on neighbourhood effects tends to focus on understanding the social and economic outcomes for people living in disadvantaged neighbourhoods when these are compared with populations in more affluent neighbourhoods. There is also often a preference for quantitative methodologies and statistical analysis, contrasting with other sociological work in poor neighbourhoods of a more qualitative nature which attempts to explore the complexity of life in these places. This latter type of study can be placed in the long tradition of community studies in both the UK and the United States,[10] some of which are discussed in the next chapter.

Harald Bauder, a geographer who authored an influential and critical paper on neighbourhood effects in 2002, argued that:

> The idea of neighbourhood effects suggests that the demographic context of poor neighbourhoods instils 'dysfunctional' norms, values and behaviours into individuals and triggers a cycle of social pathology and poverty that few residents escape.[11]

Neighbourhood effects studies claim to demonstrate that where you live affects your life chances and that 'place matters' when it comes to addressing social issues. These studies have been influential on both sides of the Atlantic partly because, as Tom Slater, a geographer at Edinburgh University, points out in a trenchant critique of the concept, 'it is seductively simple and, on the surface, very convincing'.[12] Focusing on problems caused in and by 'problem areas' is also politically expedient for politicians attempting to distract attention away from the shortcomings or unintended consequences of their own policies. Slater goes on to argue that neighbourhood effects is:

> more than a concept – it is an *instrument of accusation*, a veiled form of class antagonism that conveniently has no place for any concern over what happens *outside* the very neighbourhoods under scrutiny.[13]

William Booth suggested in 1890 that 'civilisation breeds its own barbarians', and, over a century later, Cameron argued that post-war housing estates 'entrench poverty', 'entrap families' and act as an incubator for all manner of unrelated social ills. The concept of neighbourhood effects is thus linked with the Othering thesis of the 'underclass', discussed in Chapter 1. Just as there is alleged to be a group of individuals or families who are cut off from the mainstream and who display different norms from the majority population, often passed down from their parents, there is also an alleged concentration of neighbourhoods where these people can be found, and where all people share the same morals by virtue of sharing the same physical space.

Loic Wacquant has also recently advanced the concept 'territorial stigmatisation' to describe the 'blemish of place' which is 'superimposed on already existing stigmata traditionally associated with poverty and ethnic origin or postcolonial immigrant status'.[14] Just as certain poor people become associated with alleged problematic behaviour, with little regard for structural influences, so do some poor neighbourhoods. Wacquant argues:

Advanced marginality tends to concentrate in isolated and bounded territories increasingly perceived by both outsiders and insiders as social purgatories, leprous Badlands at the heart of the postindustrial metropolis where only the refuse of society would accept to dwell.[15]

Certain neighbourhoods thus become shorthand for social problems ranging from poverty to drug dealing and violent crime. Moss Side in Manchester, Elswick in Newcastle, South Bank in Middlesbrough, Broadwater Farm in London, Chapeltown in Leeds, St Pauls in Bristol, Toxteth in Liverpool, and Shettleston and Easterhouse in Glasgow are all estates or wards of towns or cities in the UK that are associated with poverty, disorder, unrest and criminal activity, to greater or less extents. In the United States, Chicago's South Side, the Bronx in New York and South Central Los Angeles have all acquired similar reputations. There is now a wealth of literature on the deployment and effects of territorial stigmatisation across the globe, and countries such as Sweden, Denmark and the Netherlands have estates that are considered to be 'no-go areas' for many people.[16] In Denmark, there is even an official definition of what a ghetto is, and a list of neighbourhoods – popularly referred to as 'the ghetto list' – that meet the criteria is published each year by the

Danish government.[17] The extent to which these areas are 'dilapidated and dangerous' does not matter that much in the end, according to Wacquant, as 'the prejudicial belief that they are suffices to set off socially noxious consequences.'[18] Echoing Said's argument that portrayals of spaces are always representations of reality, researchers examining the different processes of territorial stigmatisation have thus argued that, across different countries, certain disadvantaged neighbourhoods

> come to be universally renowned and reviled across class and space as redoubts of self-inflicted and self-perpetuating destitution and depravity. Their names circulate in the discourses of journalism, politics and scholarship, as well as in ordinary conversations as synonyms for social hell. This sulphurous image prevails not just among social and cultural elites – as with their predecessors of a century ago – but among the citizenry at large, including those who dwell in these damned districts and those entirely removed from them.[19]

Such thinking leads to spatially targeted programmes which attempt to address the local causes of disadvantage. The last 40 or 50 years of urban policy in the UK is littered with examples of such approaches, including the Community Development Programmes of the 1970s, Urban Development Corporations in the 1980s and City Challenge in the 1990s. More recently, and under the early New Labour government of the late 1990s and early 2000s, there were Single Regeneration Budgets, New Deals for Communities, Neighbourhood Renewal Funds, Health and Education Action Zones. These initiatives slowed down during Gordon Brown's time as prime minister and came to an abrupt halt when a coalition government was formed in 2010. No specific neighbourhood policies were announced or indeed sustained by the coalition, which was obsessed by austerity and presented regeneration as a matter to be decided upon locally, in keeping with its rhetorical emphasis on localism and decentralisation. The coalition also stopped monitoring spatial inequalities, and existing public-sector-led regeneration programmes were eschewed in favour of an approach which prioritised private-sector-led economic growth.[20]

Two urban spaces in the UK that have experienced the 'blemish of place' are the Aylesbury Estate in London and Easterhouse in Glasgow. The names of these places have most definitely circulated in the discourses of journalism, politics and scholarship in recent years and have become synonymous with poverty, 'worklessness' and the 'broken society'. The elevation of these areas to sites of national interest in recent years has been helped following the patronage of two powerful politicians: Tony Blair and Iain Duncan Smith. Before discussing these efforts further, however, it is worth noting that it is possible to argue that living or growing up in disadvantaged areas can and does affect you, without leaping to deterministic conclusions about the negative nature of those effects. In her study of social housing entitled *Estates*, Lynsey Hanley refers to this as 'estatism', and the London School of Economics researcher Lisa McKenzie argues in her book *Getting By* that the effects of growing up on a council estate seep into your body in different ways.[21] Both authors avoid the pathologising tendencies of much neighbourhood effects research, and instead highlight the complexity of these effects, especially how they are negotiated by residents when they are *off* their estate.

THE AYLESBURY ESTATE AND 'THE FORGOTTEN PEOPLE'

When Tony Blair was elected prime minister in 1997, he chose the Aylesbury Estate in Southwark, London, as the setting for his first speech. Built in the 1960s and 1970s, the Aylesbury Estate replaced older Victorian housing that was considered no longer fit for purpose. The estate featured elevated walkways – 'streets in the sky' – and the early residents loved their new properties. However, according to *The Times* journalist Martin Fletcher, 'the euphoria did not last':

> The shoddily built blocks developed leaks and draughts. The lifts and heating system broke down regularly. The rubbish chutes got blocked. The stairwells and dark passages attracted junkies, prostitutes and the homeless. Empty flats were taken over by squatters or used as crack dens. Worst of all, the aerial walkways proved a paradise for muggers and burglars, offering easy access to flats and handy escape routes.[22]

Fletcher recounts how, in 1983, *The Times* reported that 'petty crime, and some not so petty, is normal';[23] there were also 'muggings in the vandalised and darkened entrance and lift areas, burglaries in the flats, even armed robberies'.[24] By the early 1990s, the police were refusing to enter the estate, especially at night. The estate was also used extensively by television and film crews in search of gritty urban locations.

So when Blair visited the Aylesbury Estate on 2 June 1997, it may have seemed a strange choice to many people. As the *Independent* noted, the new prime minister's first official speech was not to Labour Party supporters, or to a friendly think-tank policy audience or other 'elites'. It was delivered to tenants in what was referred to as 'one of the most run-down council estates in London'.[25] Blair himself was unequivocal as to why he had chosen the estate as the setting for his speech:

> I have chosen this housing estate to deliver my first speech as Prime Minister for a very simple reason. For 18 years, the poorest people in our country have been forgotten by government. They have been left out of growing prosperity, told that they were not needed, ignored by the Government except for the purpose of blaming them. I want that to change. There will be no forgotten people in the Britain I want to build.[26]

Blair stated that 'just as there are no no-go areas for new Labour so there will be no no-hope areas in new Labour's Britain'. In an act of symbolic violence, he went on to talk about the 'fatalism' and 'the dead weight of low expectations, the crushing belief that things cannot get better' that needed to be addressed if the country was to improve and succeed. The implication was clear: people on the Aylesbury Estate had given up and this lack of aspiration and hope was, as much as anything else, the reason for their poverty:

> Behind the statistics lie households where three generations have never had a job. There are estates where the biggest employer is the drugs industry, where all that is left of the high hopes of the post-war planners is derelict concrete. Behind the statistics are people who have lost hope, trapped in fatalism.

Blair talked of an 'underclass … cut off from society's mainstream' and a 'new workless class', going on to state that it was necessary to 'bring this new workless class back into society and into useful work', to 'reconnect' it and 'bring jobs, skills, opportunities and ambition to all those people who have been left behind by the Conservative years'. 'Fatalism, and not just poverty', amongst a geographically concentrated 'workless class' was 'the problem we face', according to Blair. Although the speech was delivered to residents of the estate, it was very much addressed to the wider electorate, with the location providing the perfect site to articulate the divisions in British society. Blair symbolically chose a previous 'no-go area' for his first speech, and was then photographed on an elevated concrete walkway against a backdrop of high-rise concrete flats and standing next to a police officer.

The choice of location for Blair's speech makes perfect sense once its content is considered. Drawing on Murray Edelman's work on the symbolic uses of politics, the Aylesbury Estate was an entirely appropriate 'political setting' to use for such a speech and firmly established places like the Aylesbury Estate, and the people that lived there, as challenges to national prosperity. Edelman argued that:

> Although every act takes place in a setting, we ordinarily take scenes for granted, focussing our attention on actions. When certain special kinds of acts are to take place, however, a very different practice prevails. Great pains are taken to call attention to settings and to present them conspicuously as if the scene were expected either to call forth a response of its own or to heighten the response to the act it frames.[27]

The Aylesbury Estate was instantly associated with poverty and crime in the minds of the public, many of whom would never had heard of it before, let alone been there. Denying the residents of the Aylesbury Estate the right to define themselves, Blair called them 'forgotten people' and brought them to the attention of the mainstream majority, to whom he was determined to 'reconnect' them. In choosing the Aylesbury Estate as the location for his speech, Blair, who spoke of the dangers of institutionalising poverty, attempted to localise the causes of it.

EASTERHOUSE AND THE 'DAMASCENE' MOMENT

Tony Blair was not the first politician to choose a disadvantaged area to make a political statement, and nor was he the last. In 2002, the then leader of the Conservative Party, Iain Duncan Smith, travelled to Easterhouse in Glasgow in an attempt to demonstrate that he wanted to 'listen and learn' from the people that Blair had accused the Tories of 'forgetting'.[28] His visit was referred to as the 'Easterhouse Epiphany' by the Scottish newspaper the *Herald*, and Duncan Smith himself later admitted that it was 'a sort of Damascene point'.[29]

Subsequent visits to Easterhouse and other parts of the East End of Glasgow helped to bring Duncan Smith 'back from the land of the political dead' following a disastrous spell as leader of the Conservatives.[30] It was during these visits that he allegedly discovered his 'passion for social justice'. Once again, the setting seems entirely appropriate for a politician attempting to mark himself out as a 'champion' of and for the poor. The *Daily Telegraph* noted, in keeping with the 'forgotten people', discourse that, 'IDS went to streets that had seen few Tories in recent years, to find out what causes poverty and how to put it right',[31] whilst an influential right-wing blog stated that, as a result of the visits, 'Duncan Smith's moral standing remains somehow unassailable'.[32] The community organiser Bob Holman, who first invited Duncan Smith to Easterhouse but later changed his opinion of him, stated that he 'almost wept at the plight of the poor' and possessed a 'rare gift of being able to listen to and communicate with people crushed by social deprivation'.[33] Duncan Smith was photographed outside boarded-up flats, looking glumly into the distance. This, the images told us, was a man troubled by what he saw.

Duncan Smith established the Centre for Social Justice (CSJ) following a promise he made to Janis Dobbie, a woman he met in Easterhouse, whose son had just died following a heroin overdose.[34] Duncan Smith's frequent visits helped ensure that Easterhouse and other parts of east Glasgow became strongly associated with the concept of a dysfunctional and 'broken society'. The *Daily Telegraph* stated that in Easterhouse it was not unemployment that was the problem, but 'chronic anemployment', associated with 'a criminal underclass' and 'people who think that they have a hereditary right to live off benefits; families in which no male has had a job for three generations'.[35] In 2008, the CSJ published a report which drew attention to what it called 'Shettleston Man', referring to male residents of another deprived area of east Glasgow, and bringing to mind prehistoric or primitive groups such as Peking Man, Java Man or Neanderthal Man:

Shettleston Man is the collective name given for a group of men in Shettleston. Shettleston Man's life expectancy is 63, he lives in social housing and is terminally out of work. His white blood cell count is killing him due to the stress of living in deprivation.[36]

Duncan Smith himself stated that it was going to Glasgow that helped him realise the scale of the problems that society faced and, indeed, what had caused them:

> Standing in the middle of an estate like Easterhouse, you know it was built after the war for a purpose, only to see this wrecked and dreadful set-up today, with families locked into generational breakdown, poverty, drug addiction and so on. And that really does confront you with the thought that we did this – we built the brave new world, and look where it's gone.[37]

When David Cameron took over the leadership of the Conservatives in 2006, he appointed Duncan Smith as the head of a social justice policy group, for which the CSJ acted as secretariat. Cameron frequently spoke up in support of Duncan Smith, and even referred to him as the greatest social justice champion the Tories had ever had. Cameron, as noted previously, even branded a by-election in Glasgow East in 2008 as the 'broken society by-election'. The Tories did not win the by-election, but they did go on to form a coalition government with the Liberal Democrats following the 2010 general election. Duncan Smith was appointed secretary of state for work and pensions, tasked with overhauling the welfare state which allegedly allowed, if not encouraged, poverty, 'worklessness' and various associated ills to fester in disadvantaged neighbourhoods. His own and the government's response, as will be discussed in Chapter 8, was to push through a wide range of public sector and welfare 'reforms' that hit the poorest families and the poorest areas hardest.

WESTMINSTER EFFECTS

The idea of 'sink estates', no-go areas and 'problem neighbourhoods' that create and exacerbate their own problems have a long history that has not been fully explored here. This chapter has, however, examined some recent interventions by politicians in the UK in debates about the causes of and solutions to the geographic concentration of poverty and deprivation in certain urban areas. Tony Blair and Iain Duncan Smith, interlopers from Westminster, both used poor, working-class communities as the backdrop to their political statements or moves designed to make them stand out – or gain distinction – from other politicians. This distinction was gained by visiting places that had been 'forgotten about' by politicians, and that would be 'unrecognisable' to people living in the cleaner, less defiled suburbs. Blair visited the Aylesbury Estate to give his symbolically important first speech as prime minister, and Duncan Smith made a series of visits to Easterhouse and other parts of east Glasgow as part of an attempt to recreate himself as politician of conviction and with a 'passion for social justice'.

Just as Lyndon Johnson visited poor communities in America in the 1960s and acted 'right down to earth' and 'just like a neighbour', Blair and Duncan Smith, in visiting impoverished estates, were attempting to benefit from what Pierre Bourdieu called 'strategies of condescension', whereby dominant and powerful individuals attempt to 'symbolically deny the social distance between themselves and others'.[38] By taking part in activities that make one look 'down to earth' and 'not stand off-ish', such as visiting poor areas and talking to people living in poverty, politicians and other 'important' people attempt to gain distinction from their peers and 'cumulate the advantages of propinquity and the advantages of distance, that is, distance and the recognition of distance warranted by its symbolic denegation'.[39] Whilst Cameron's sink-estates speech certainly gained headlines, it was interesting that he chose to give his speech at the children's charity Family Action and not at one of the estates he was talking about, thereby potentially limiting the symbolic impact of the speech. Perhaps his experience in Benchill, in Wythenshawe, south Manchester, in 2007, when he was photographed with a young male behind him wearing a 'hoodie' and pointing an imaginary gun at Cameron using his fingers, had made him more cautious in choosing the political settings he was prepared to speak at.[40]

The intense focus on a small number of spatially peripheral problem or bad neighbourhoods 'located elsewhere' leads to 'phantasms, which feed on emotional experiences stimulated by more or less uncontrolled words and images, such as those conveyed in the tabloids and by political propaganda and rumour'.[41] Stigmatised spaces appear to take on a life of their own, able to 'entrench poverty' and 'attract disadvantage'. Residents are portrayed as members of a homogeneous underclass, and the reality of neighbourhoods as contested, heterogeneous spaces gets glossed over by this simplistic narrative. Such myths also deflect attention away from the external forces that largely determine the conditions in which people live.

Families in Easterhouse and the Aylesbury Estate are not responsible for housing policy, nor do they decide macro-economic policy, wage levels or education systems or structures. Residents do not make decisions about the levels of support offered via what is supposed to be a system of social security, nor do they have much influence over the levels of funding available to local public services. People living in poor neighbourhoods do not even have much say over how they are talked about or treated by such services and other organisations and institutions. They generally do not generate their own stigmatisation. The 'taint of place' that is often attached to working-class neighbourhoods comes from the representation of those areas in media and political discourses.

Decisions about resources and services that could be made available to neighbourhoods and their residents are often taken hundreds of miles away, perhaps by people whose only experience or knowledge of poverty might have been gleaned from a carefully managed day trip or two. It is worth remembering that few, if any, of the politicians who voted through, or abstained during, the welfare reforms introduced in the UK since 2010, were going to be substantially affected by them, or could imagine what they might mean to many families already living on low incomes across the country. Economic geographers working at the Centre for Regional Economic and Social Research at Sheffield Hallam University have demonstrated various 'Westminster effects' on disadvantaged neighbourhoods by highlighting how the government's recent welfare reforms have had disproportionately greater impact upon poorer areas.[42] In a similar vein, researchers at the Institute for Fiscal Studies have demonstrated that it is poorer local authorities that lost most money from central government changes to local government spending and revenue allocation.[43] More recently, in December 2016, the Department for Education announced a new funding formula for schools that would see funding shift from many schools in poorer, urban areas to often more affluent rural areas in the south and east of England.[44]

Whilst it is vital to acknowledge that where people live can significantly affect their lives, a compelling case can be made that the strongest effects, both symbolic and material, exerted on residents of disadvantaged neighbourhoods in the UK often emanate from the words and actions of politicians in Westminster, rather than emerging out of concrete walkways.

5
Streetwise?

[M]ean streets produce mean men, tired women, and dirty children.

John Burns, 1910.[1]

There are few more symbolically powerful or evocative geographies – real or imagined – than 'the street'. Many people grow up living in houses on streets, and spend a great deal of time playing 'in the street' as children or 'hanging around' or wandering them as teenagers. People's lives are often presented as being organised around, or even by, the interactions and relations they have on their street. These views have been augmented by popular British soap operas such as *Coronation Street*, *Brookside* and *EastEnders*, which focus on the relationships and tensions that occur in residential micro-spaces such as streets, cul-de-sacs and squares, as well as American and Canadian children's television shows such as *Sesame Street* and *Degrassi Street*. There is also a 'darker' side to the street, with references to 'mean streets', problematic 'street cultures' and deviant 'ways of the street'.

In America, street corners have a similar resonance. Corners of blocks are places where pedestrian crossings are usually located, where main thoroughfares and boulevards carrying commuters and assorted 'outsiders' intersect with local streets and residents whose travel options are more limited. Entrances and exits for the Subway are found on some corners. They are where formal businesses such as bars, liquor stores, grocery stores and laundromats are located, and where informal, sometimes illegal, businesses emerge and illicit trades take place. In the popular American crime series, *The Wire*, set in Baltimore, Avon Barksdale, a successful drug dealer, highlights the symbolic importance of 'corners' when he rejects the opportunity to leave his corners behind and become a 'legitimate' businessman by stating, 'You know, I'm just a gangsta, I suppose. *And I want my corners*'. Corners, then, are liminal and symbolically potent spaces where threats and opportunities can be found.

In some ethnographic research, there has often been a strong focus on describing and illuminating 'the street' and an interest in the activities and routines of 'street corner society'. Researchers have studied 'street oriented' families and 'street-present' youth, documented various types of 'street culture' and revealed the 'code of the street'. At the same time, other researchers have arguably adopted what the American public policy and management scholar Evelyn Brodkin has called a 'street-level lens', which 'provides strategies for investigating questions of common interest located at the intersection of fields'.[2] Writing about the implementation of public policies by 'street-level bureaucrats' – the frontline workers of the state such as police officers, social workers, youth workers, welfare officers and housing officers – Brodkin argues that the 'central task' of a 'street-level lens' 'is to expose the informal practices through which policies – and by extension social politics and social relations – are effectively negotiated'.[3] The concept 'street-level lens' is, I believe, equally applicable to street-level research that studies the daily routines and practices of members of the public, and the 'social politics and social relations' that influence and exert pressures on them, as much as it applies to paid officers tasked with implementing public policies.

An alternative way of contrasting the two approaches is to consider the first, street-focused method as equivalent to 'thick description', and the latter method as being more akin to 'thick construction'. The anthropologist Clifford Geertz famously argued that the anthropologist and other ethnographers were pursuing descriptions that could reveal:

> a multiplicity of complex conceptual structures, many of them superimposed upon or knotted into one another, which are at once strange, irregular, and inexplicit, and which he [sic] must contrive somehow first to grasp and then to render.[4]

This is not the place to examine Geertz's work in detail. The book, a collection of his own essays, where he originally set out the concept, has been cited over 8,000 times. It is however, worth noting that whilst Geertz advocated 'microscopic' research practice, he was also very clear about the limits of such research and argued that localised findings should not be extrapolated in a 'Jonesville-is-the-USA' microcosmic way.[5] He was sceptical of the idea that ethnographic studies could present 'the world in a teacup',[6] and he believed that the notion that such research was able to elevate its practitioners to 'some moral vantage ground from which you can look down upon the ethically less privileged' was 'an idea which only someone too long in the bush could possibly entertain'.[7] Geertz did, however, suggest that signs, symbols and behaviours witnessed up close could be used in an attempt to interpret and understand wider themes and events. He argued that 'social actions are comments on more than themselves' and that '[s]mall facts speak to large issues'.[8]

Loic Wacquant has, in recent years, proposed an alternative conceptualisation of ethnographic research. In opposition to Geertz's 'thick description', Wacquant has argued for ethnographic research to provide a 'thick construction' of life amongst impoverished communities.[9] The difference is subtle, but important. Whilst the former focuses attention on describing and explaining what can be observed, the latter offers up the opportunity of focusing attention more on the deeper social and political structures that shape life in local spaces.

In this chapter, then, researchers that use and describe 'the street' when studying poverty, inequality and marginalisation are themselves the subject of investigation. The chapter attempts to highlight differences between researchers that focus on 'the street' as well and those that use a 'street-level lens' to study wider social structures. Firstly, the extensive and influential work of American sociologist Elijah Anderson and street criminologists in the UK and Europe who draw on his work is critiqued. Attention then turns to sociologists in the United States and the UK who have used street-level research to examine and understand wider changes and structural shifts in society as a whole. The chapter concludes with further discussion of the benefits of researchers linking 'mean streets' with wider societal values.

A FOCUS ON THE STREET

Sociologists at the University of Chicago were encouraged to view their city as a 'living laboratory' from the 1920s onwards, and forays into disadvantaged neighbourhoods produced a number of influential publications on street populations such as Nels Anderson's *The Hobo*, W.I. Thomas's *The Unadjusted Girl* and Frederick Thrasher's *The Gang*.[10] Other case studies of delinquent young people and young offenders along with ethnographies of urban neighbourhoods followed, including William Foote Whyte's seminal work *Street Corner Society*.[11] The opening paragraph of this book highlights why areas such as 'Cornerville' attracted the attention of researchers;

In the heart of 'Eastern City' there is a slum district known as Cornerville, which is inhabited almost exclusively by Italian immigrants and their children. To the rest of the city it is a mysterious, dangerous, and depressing area. Cornerville is only a few minutes' walk from fashionable High Street, but the High Street inhabitant who takes that walk passes from the familiar to the unknown.[12]

Whyte highlighted how 'respectable people' had limited contact with the inhabitants of Cornerville and similar districts, and were often reliant on official statistics and media reports to acquire knowledge about the areas. Such information, Whyte argued, was always incomplete, if not incorrect or biased.[13] According to Whyte, the only way to 'acquire the most intimate knowledge of local life' was to carry out ethnographic research, virtually living in Cornerville and immersing oneself in the daily activities, routines and customs of the people that resided there. Subsequently, a number of other influential studies of disadvantaged neighbourhoods sought to examine life on 'the street' or at 'the corner'. One of the most well-known 'street sociologists' is the black American academic, Elijah Anderson, who has written extensively about the residents of marginalised neighbourhoods in a number of works, including the books *A Place on the Corner*, *Streetwise* and *Code of the Street*.[14]

His book *A Place on the Corner* focuses on 'Jelly's', a bar and liquor store on the corner of a main thoroughfare in the South Side of Chicago. Anderson spent a great deal of time talking to people, mainly black men, either unemployed or in low-paid, insecure work, who frequented Jelly's. He describes his encounters and his observations in great detail and establishes different categories of street-corner men at Jelly's: the regulars, the wineheads and the hoodlums.

In *Streetwise*, Anderson again used ethnographic methods to understand an area he calls Village-Northon, which included two distinct communities: one racially mixed, middle-class neighbourhood, and one poor and primarily black neighbourhood. Anderson highlights that he:

spent many hours on the streets ... videotaped street corner scenes ... got to know all kinds of people from small-time drug dealers to policemen, middle class whites, and outspoken black community activists [and] frequented neighbourhood bars, laundromats, and carryouts and attended brunches, parties and community gatherings.[15]

In the book, Anderson introduces the concepts of 'street wisdom' and 'street etiquette'.[16] He argues that 'a "streetwise" person is one who understands "how to behave" in uncertain public places' and is able to understand 'the give and take of street life'.[17] 'Street etiquette', however, 'requires only a generalised perception of the people one encounters, based on the most superficial characteristics'.[18] The streets, then, according to Anderson, are full of danger – usually emanating from 'street-smart young boys', 'street kids' and 'street blacks', all of whom are usually 'products of the street gang'.[19]

In *The Code of the Street*, Anderson identifies two different types of families – employing labels used by residents of poor neighbourhoods: 'decent families' and 'street families'. In decent families, according to Anderson:

> there is almost always a real concern with and a certain amount of hope for the future. Such attitudes are often expressed in a drive to work 'to have something' or 'to build a good life', while at the same time trying to 'make do with what you have'. This means working hard, saving money for material things, and raising children – any 'child you touch' – to try to make something out of themselves.[20]

Decent families are thus associated with all things wholesome and mainstream: they instil children with 'backbone' and a sense of responsibility; they are more likely to go to church and engage with schools; they value hard work and the 'man of the house' is seen as a respectable figure and 'the head of the household'.[21] In contrast, street families:

> often show a lack of consideration for other people and have a rather superficial sense of family and community. They may love their children but frequently find it difficult both to cope with the physical and emotional demands of parenthood and to reconcile their needs with those of their children. Members of these families, who are more fully invested in the code of the street than the decent people are, may aggressively socialise their children into it in a normative way. They more fully believe in the code and judge themselves and others according to its values.[22]

Anderson provides vignettes of both decent and street families, with people's lives, relationships and public encounters described in great detail. The focus of Anderson's writing is, across all three books, on the comings and goings of 'the street'. So, for example, in *Code of the Street*, we learn all about Dickens, whose wife, according to local rumour, allowed her crack habit to get out of control before becoming a prostitute to raise funds for her addiction. Dickens's day apparently begins at around 11 a.m. when he ventures out for cheese-steaks and videos for his 'visitors'. His children are allowed to 'rip and run' up and down the street, often unsupervised and at all hours of the day and night, whilst their father listens to loud music, plays cards and drinks beer with his friends, often on the porch. His neighbours suspect he is a crack dealer.[23]

This focus on the minutiae of street life is often at the expense of discussions about wider structural forces that impact on poor black neighbourhoods in the USA. At times, then, with the simplistic separation of poverty-stricken families into 'street' and 'decent', and with lurid discussions of 'street-oriented women [who] are crack-addicted ("on the pipe"), alcoholic, or involved in complicated relationships with men who abuse them',[24] Anderson seems intent on 'proving' the existence of a violent, pathological black underclass in America. The novel separation of 'the poor' into 'deserving' and 'undeserving' categories has been challenged robustly by Wacquant, who acknowledges that whilst Anderson points out that these are the residents' own labels, not his, he then bases his argument around them and does little to interrogate the concepts.[25]

Sociologists of deviance, from the 1950s onwards, have highlighted how labelling people as deviant in some way (such as 'street families' or 'troubled families', or individuals who are 'mentally ill' and so forth) may lead those people to become (more) deviant, thus behaving in the way that society expects them to.[26] Being labelled by professionals or neighbours denies individuals and families the opportunity to forge positive identities for themselves. Anderson thus appears to accept the labels of 'street' and 'decent' families as empirical realities and offers up his own vision of divisions, whereby residents of poor black neighbourhoods can be neatly divided into two groups. These are precisely the readily available folk concepts applied to marginalised populations that should be rejected by sociologists and other social researchers. Instead, Anderson embraces them, weaving them into his narrative about 'the code of the street', providing the labels with a credibility that they do not deserve.

Outside the United States, a number of criminologists have similarly focused on 'street life' and 'street culture', and have deployed concepts inspired by the work of Pierre Bourdieu to examine the activities and routines of young people involved in 'the street field'. The Norwegian criminologist Sveinung Sandberg, for example, has advanced the concept of 'street capital' – the skills, competencies and dispositions necessary to survive as a lower-level drug dealer – to examine the daily struggles of and competition between ethnic minority young people on the streets of Oslo.[27]

In the UK, the criminologist Simon Harding, a former civil servant in the Home Office, has also used the term 'street capital' and written about 'the street casino' and 'street government' in his research on gangs in London.[28] Harding argues that gang members and their associates are striving to become 'players in the game' in the 'casino of life', with success determined by the amount of 'chips' they can accrue. In his book *The Street Casino*, Harding manages to combine a healthy dose of underclass theory with a large dollop of territorial stigmatisation. It opens as follows:

> The social field of the gang in London SW9 is a dangerous arena of social conflict and competition for some young people.
>
> While gang researchers struggle to articulate this domain, or to even acknowledge it, the young men and women within it live a daily reality that remains largely remote, and, for many adults, estranged, inexplicable and impenetrable. It is a world where social norms are inverted; where rumour and gossip lead to death and injury; where personal slights become 'beefs', then feuds; where family members are fair game for reprisals; where boys are 'soljas' and dead age 15.[29]

In discussing the role of 'street gangs' in the 2011 riots in England, Harding argues that the gangs represent a 'form of street government' in deprived neighbourhoods where public forms of authority have retreated.[30] He draws on Anderson's *Code of the Street* and suggests that a 'governance vacuum' has occurred in 'difficult to manage' urban areas.[31] The concept of 'street government' sounds perilously close to David Cameron's representation of post-war housing estates as 'sink estates' that are 'cut off, self-governing and divorced from the mainstream'.[32] Once again, sociological or criminological research that focuses on 'thick descriptions' of 'the street' appears to risk doing little more than ratifying existing or official 'social problems' and should therefore be treated with caution.

A STREET-LEVEL LENS

There are, however, alternative approaches to carrying out and interpreting the data produced and collected during street-based research. The approaches described above often focus on the street and view it as a society in its own right, with, for example, its own 'government', often different in certain ways from wider society. Other researchers have decided instead to use street-level research as a lens through which to understand the impact of wider structural forces. They have thus attached less symbolic importance to 'the street' itself.

In his book *Urban Outcasts*, for example, Loic Wacquant manages to provide a compelling account, based on ethnographic research, of social exclusion and what he calls 'advanced marginality' in capitalist societies whilst barely mentioning 'the street' at all.[33] His analysis instead focuses on the social and economic policies that have, he argues, resulted in the withdrawal of the state and other institutions from poor black neigh-bourhoods in the United States, rather than the putative emergence of a black 'underclass' in explaining the 'advanced marginality' he observed. Although no formal distinction is made between the two ethnographic approaches of focusing on the street or using a 'street-level lens' (nor am I suggesting there should be, given that they would be 'false oppositions'), they potentially offer very different perspectives on the lives of residents who frequent the streets and street corners.

In a recent reissue of the American anthropologist Elliot Liebow's classic study, *Tally's Corner*, the eminent sociologist Charles Lemert asserts that the book 'is a story of the Black man in the city told *from the point of view of social structures*'.[34] In the main body of the text, Liebow sets out how he collected his data, and the similarities with Anderson are notable. Liebow spent around 18 months in the field and states that data were collected during 'all hours of day and night'.[35] The majority of the material in the book was drawn from a small group of black men who frequented a corner in Washington and used it as a 'base of operations'.[36] Many of these men were employed in insecure, low level, unskilled work of different types, although at various times throughout the study many were also unemployed. Liebow also states that, whilst the main body of data 'comprises a record of the day-to-day routines' of the men on the corner, following them around alleys, pool rooms, houses and 'beer joints' in the vicinity of the corner, these men also ventured further afield:

> Frequently ... associations which began on the streetcorner led me out of the neighbourhood to courtrooms, jails, hospitals, dance halls, beaches and private houses elsewhere in Washington, Maryland and Virginia.[37]

In doing so, Liebow establishes that the street-corner men remain connected to wider society and its institutions in different, if not always entirely unproblematic, ways. These men were not, therefore, members of a class or group that is 'cut off' from the mainstream majority. Liebow also notes that the street-corner men he studied are 'not in any strict sense, a group'.[38] He highlights that many are 'poor, dependent, delinquent', but immediately asserts that, at the same time, many are not, and their living standards vary greatly. Liebow also acknowledges the diversity that exists in the wider neighbourhood, stating that not all men who live in the neighbourhood can be found or seen on the corner:

> The man who lives up the street from the Carry-out and works two or three jobs to keep his home and family together may divide all his waking time between home and job. Such a man may be unknown at the Carry-out and at other public places in the area.[39]

Liebow manages to avoid the simplistic labelling of families or men in or around Tally's Corner as one thing or the other. Throughout the book, he continues to highlight how 'outside' pressures and structures affect the daily lives of residents 'inside' the neighbourhood. In a discussion of the employment conditions and opportunities of the men on the corner, he recounts a story of a pickup-truck driver who stops on streets and at various corners in the neighbourhood looking for casual labourers, with little success, despite an abundance of men with no gainful employment of their own. Liebow rhetorically asks if we have witnessed 'lazy, irresponsible men turning down an honest day's pay for an honest day's work' or a 'more complex phenomenon marking the intersection of economic forces, social values and individual states of mind and body?'[40] Liebow then highlights the diversity of reasons why men refuse the work offered, including: having other ad-hoc commitments and appointments that need to be kept; being in employment at night or enjoying a day off; finding illegal ways of making money; a 'don't work and don't want to work minority'; construction or physically demanding jobs being beyond the capacity of some of the men; and the low pay and the low value that is attached to many of the jobs. He explicates the implications of this last reason in a paragraph that is worth quoting in full:

> For his part, the streetcorner man puts no lower value on the job than does the larger society around him. He knows the social value of the job by the amount of money the employer is willing to pay him for doing it. In a real sense, every pay day, he counts in dollars and cents the value placed on a job by society at large. He is no more (and frequently less) ready to quit and look for another job than his employer is ready to fire him and look for another man. Neither the streetcorner man who performs these jobs nor the society which requires him to perform them assess the job as one 'worth doing and worth doing well'. Both employee and employer are contemptuous of the job. The employee shows his contempt by his reluctance to accept it or keep it, the employer by paying less than is required to support a family. Nor does the low-wage job offer prestige, respect, interesting work, opportunity for learning or advancement, or any other compensation. With few exceptions, jobs filled by the streetcorner men are at the bottom of the employment ladder in every respect, from wage level to prestige. Typically, they are hard, dirty, uninteresting and underpaid. The rest of society (whatever its ideal values regarding the dignity of labour) holds the job of the dishwasher or janitor or unskilled labourer in low esteem if not outright contempt. So does the streetcorner man. He cannot do otherwise. He cannot draw from a job those social values which other people do not put into it.[41]

In his concluding chapter, Liebow argues that the street corner he studies 'did not appear as a self-contained, self-generating, self-sustaining system ... with clear boundaries marking it off from the larger world around it'.[42] Instead, he argued that it was an integral part of the larger society and was in 'continuous, intimate contact' with it.[43] This focus on street-level comings and goings 'from the point of view of social structures', as Lemert called it, provides an exemplar of what a street-level lens or a thick-construction approach can achieve, in contrast to a thinner, narrower perspective that focuses more on the detail of micro-encounters and interactions.

In the UK there has been less focus on the symbolic spaces of 'the street' or 'the corner' in sociological and geographical research, which has arguably tended to be more interested in 'the community' and 'the neighbourhood'. This may have something to do with the fact that a street presence in the UK is associated more with young people and transitions from childhood to adulthood than with the mixed ages and adults associated with street life in the United States. In this context, the sociologists Tracy Shildrick, Robert Macdonald and colleagues' discussions of 'street corner society' in their Teesside studies are useful in examining the wider processes of deindustrialisation and social exclusion.[44] In Robert Macdonald and Jane Marsh's book *Disconnected Youth?*, a chapter on the 'leisure careers' of young people explores the ways in which they are prevented from accessing other, more 'acceptable' leisure pursuits through a lack of resources, and how the reality of teenagers hanging around the streets is often far more mundane than many adults would have us believe.[45] Too old, in the young people's own eyes, for youth clubs, and without the financial resources that secure employment brings, the young people making the transition from childhood to adulthood in the Teesside studies gravitate towards the liminal space of the street where they attempt to be (relatively) free of adult scrutiny. Fittingly, and acknowledging wider influences than 'the street' on the lives of these young people, the chapter sits between other discussions of youth transitions: training opportunities, housing options, the possibility of finding work and the implications of becoming a young parent.

This simultaneous focus on wider – historical, cultural and political – determinants of 'street life' and 'street corner society' can also be found in other British studies. Owen Gill's book *Luke Street*, which includes a chapter on 'The Boys on Casey's Corner', has the subtitle *Housing Policy, Conflict and the Creation of the Delinquent Area*.[46] Casey's is the local pub that Gill argues was the focal point of the neighbourhood and which acted as a meeting point for all the groups in the neighbourhood. In the preface, Gill notes how a study that originally intended to examine the lifestyle of a group of boys in a local area changed when he was 'drawn into issues of housing policy, policing and urban stereotyping in an attempt to understand the production of the behaviour that comes to be officially registered as delinquent'.[47]

Gill argues that the lives of the boys on Casey's Corner should not be viewed as detached or separate from the wider context of the neighbourhood and the issues that other residents faced or experienced. He acknowledges, in a similar vein to Liebow, that the focus on a group on a corner may make that group appear to be more homogeneous than it actually was. Again, the lack of employment and the insecurity of most potential jobs, added to the experience of older family members and the stigma attached to being from Luke Street, had an impact on the way the boys viewed their future prospects:

> In Casey's they could see the unemployed older brother of twenty-five and the unemployed father of forty-five. And through this contact with older unemployed men they had come to see a possible pattern for their own lives. But the boys did not suffer simply from the general difficulty of finding work. They came from an area which they believed was discriminated against in the job market and some of them faced the added difficulties of being unable to find work because of the time they had spent in correctional institutions. The cumulative effect of all these factors was the unemployment had come to be regarded as the norm and a norm that it was no use fighting against.[48]

This 'taint of place' is explored further in *Luke Street*, and Gill highlights the impact of negative local news coverage of the area and how professionals such as probation officers, social workers, youth workers, police and housing officials all regarded Luke Street as 'a "problem" area'.[49]

More recently, Lisa McKenzie has carried out extensive ethnographic research on St Ann's estate in Nottingham to examine the effects of austerity, welfare reform, stigma, racism and deepening class inequality in British society to understand the effects of these forces on residents' lives.[50] There is a single entry on 'street life',[51] but much more detail on the stigma associated with living on St Ann's and the particular high visibility of the women in the neighbourhoods who 'live in the public sphere of government agencies, schools, healthcare' and by virtue of the fact that they move around the estate with their children.[52] McKenzie highlights the women's 'acute awareness' of how they are viewed by people who do not live on the estate: 'they explain how "others" think they are "rough and ready". This term was used by many of the women in explaining how they thought "others" saw them, "rough" meaning violent, aggressive, and dirty, while "ready" means sexually available'.[53]

In Glasgow, Ali Fraser has deployed the concept of 'street habitus' to explore the deep-seated place attachment of young people in his study and to 'problematise universalist assumptions relating to youth "gangs" and territory, and emphasise the need for situated accounts that engage with historical, structural and cultural forces'.[54] Fraser's deployment of the concept of habitus to problematise dominant discourses of young people in gangs stands in marked contrast to Harding's use of Bourdieu's framework to 'shore up' the dominant depiction in the UK of young urban black men as violent gangsters. Such a contrast demonstrates that similar issues of marginality and/or criminality can be approached in very different ways by researchers, and that the perspectives offered often lead to research that offers very different interpretations and end results.

MEAN SOCIETY?

Ethnographic approaches offer up a number of opportunities for researchers interested in understanding the daily lives, routines and customs of specific communities or populations. Street-based research has often been used to gain a better insight into the daily lives of the residents of disadvantaged neighbourhoods who are often seen as 'different' in certain respects to more affluent or middle-class communities. Researchers carrying out such work can arguably make a choice about the focus of the research, and the direction in which they train their gaze. Some researchers, such as Elijah Anderson and Simon Harding, focus more on the details and intricacies of 'street life' to the detriment of a longer or 'thicker' construction of the factors and forces that influence that 'street life'.

The 'thick descriptions' examined here have tended to highlight the deviant and 'problematic' side of life on a low income. Violence, sexual promiscuity, drug dealing and drug taking, gang membership and prostitution are all issues that have been described in great detail by criminologists and sociologists of the street. In some cases, as in the example of a 'street casino', these issues risk being gratuitously glamourised. The everyday experiences of families appear to be of secondary importance to activities and events that mark sub-sections of poor communities out as being Other. Other researchers, discussed in the second half of the chapter here, such as Liebow, Shildrick and Macdonald and colleagues, and McKenzie, choose, or are able, to use 'street life' as a lens through which to view developments and changes in wider society. It is important to be clear that ethnographic research per se is not a problem. But the ends to which it is put can be problematic.

Detailed ethnographic accounts can help to shed light on the daily lives of different populations, whether they are disadvantaged or not. But when they present these populations or communities as 'cut off' or 'distinct' or Other from wider society, or do not make the links between how one influences the other and vice versa, researchers can fall into the trap of portraying 'street-oriented' individuals as members of a pathological, criminally inclined underclass. This, especially in the United States, is often associated with black communities. Too much emphasis on activities on 'the street' can thus play into a simplistic narrative that advances visible and 'problematic' behaviour such as drug addiction, alcohol abuse, domestic incompetence, workshy attitudes and parental failings as the primary causes of poverty. People may well believe that 'mean streets produce mean men, tired women, and dirty children', as the English trade unionist John Burns argued in the early years of the twentieth century, but it is surely then necessary to ask, if this is the case, what is it that produces 'mean streets' in the first place? If we do not accept the view that people living in impoverished neighbourhoods and congregating on street corners are 'cut off' from wider society, we must then acknowledge the role that society at large might play in producing some of the behaviour witnessed amongst various populations. Where wider society ascribes little value and offers little help or hope to people who spend some of their time on 'the street' – be they street-corner men or young people excluded from expensive leisure activities – preferring instead to gaze on and amplify alleged difference over obvious commonality, we should perhaps begin to interrogate the notion of a 'mean society' to go alongside the better known idea of 'mean streets'.

6

The Heroic Simplification
of the Household

Researchers into working-class dietary [*sic*] have recognised that the ordinary housewife spends her money as well as it can be spent to keep her family housed, warmed and free from hunger. Below a certain level in the population, however, and it may be that the line of demarcation is often that dividing the regular from the casual workers – there is exploitation, ignorance and waste, while at all levels housewives could be assisted to make their money go further.

Women's Group on Public Welfare, 1943.[1]

Efforts to address concentrated poverty in poor neighbourhoods and to 'regenerate' such neighbourhoods often involve the removal and relocation of entire households, with the intention of replacing them with more affluent 'non-poor' households in order to create 'mixed communities'. Such an approach essentially relies on the view that poverty can often be cured by some form of social osmosis whereby poor households' material circumstances improve by virtue of the fact that they live next to better-off households. Where there are concerns about 'anti-social', 'problem' or 'troubled' families, there is a long history in the UK, and other countries, of temporarily moving the family into residential accommodation for intensive supervision and 'retraining' before being allowed home again.[2] Whilst there are extensive, often critical, literatures on both of these approaches, they are not the focus of this chapter.

Instead, this chapter focuses on the extent to which the use of 'the household' as the level at which poverty is officially measured is problematic. Whilst headlines are often about the numbers of people or, more usually, children, living in poverty, these are figures deduced from studies of households living in poverty. We may know that around 2.5 million children are living in poverty in the UK in 2016,[3] and it is estimated that this figure will rise to around 3.5 million by 2020, but these figures are based on research which examines household incomes.[4] It is household income that is generally used, along with the size and type of households (pensioners, couples with no children, lone parents with one child, couples with two children and so on) in poverty-related research around the world. In the UK, this research, based on household surveys, is reported in the annual government publications concerning households below the average income.[5]

A number of criticisms regarding this approach have been highlighted and discussed in social policy circles for over 50 years, but they rarely make it into the wider public domain.[6] This chapter examines the way in which, when measuring and reporting poverty, a focus on the imagined geography of 'the household' in general and certain types of household more specifically make assumptions about the distribution and control of resources within the household. It invites value judgements on how household income should be spent, excludes many marginalised groups from poverty statistics and has implications for the types of policies which are advanced to tackle poverty. The chapter concludes with a discussion of how these issues could be addressed.

ASSUMPTIONS

The most common concern about measuring poverty at the household level is that it assumes equitable distribution of a household's income among members of that household. Such an assumption leads to everyone in the household being viewed as equally deprived if household income is not sufficient to allow all members of the household access to the types of activities and products that most other people in society take for granted. The famous economist J.K. Galbraith called this a 'heroic simplification', whereby 'the separate identities of men and women are merged into the concept of the household', ensuring that 'the inner conflicts and compromises of the household are not explored'.[7]

There are numerous, fairly obvious issues with this 'heroic simplification'. The main one is that the distribution of low or inadequate income within households is unlikely to be entirely equitable. The often gendered mismatch between control of money and the day-to-day management of it is well documented; men are also more likely, for a number of historical, cultural and structural reasons, to be the main earners in the household. In summary, whether the money in a household goes into, and/or remains, in the 'wallet or the purse' is often a key question in determining the extent to which its members are protected, to a greater or lesser extent, from the effects of poverty.[8]

For example, there is a body of evidence, stretching back to the work of Charles Booth and Seebohm Rowntree in Victorian and Edwardian times, that women and children are often the most deprived members of a household because of attempts, by the mother, to protect their husbands and fathers from the effects of poverty. In 1913, Rowntree wrote:

> The women and children suffer from underfeeding to a much greater extent than men. It is tacitly agreed that the man must have a certain minimum of food in order that he may be able to perform the muscular work demanded of him; and the provision of this minimum, in the case of families with small incomes involves a degree of underfeeding for the women and children greater than is shown by the average figures we present.[9]

More recently, research and reports continue to provide evidence that many mothers in low-income families miss meals in order to ensure that their children are able to eat. In 1969, the social policy researcher Hilary Land highlighted in her book *Large Families in London* that many women went without breakfast and had just a sandwich for lunch, 1 in 12 never had a cooked meal and boys were often given more food than girls.[10] Today, the increase in numbers of people relying on food banks and the issue of 'school holiday hunger' has brought this issue to the fore in the UK.[11]

Chris Warburton-Brown, an anti-poverty campaigner from Newcastle-upon-Tyne, examined how women in low-income families managed their money.[12] He states that the need to prove oneself a 'good mother', feelings of guilt and a constant struggle to make ends meet were common themes amongst the women he interviewed, along with psychological distress and worry about male financial irresponsibility.[13] The following quotation from Karen, one of his research participants, sums up a number of these issues, as well as highlighting the sacrifices made by mothers, the potential for male control of 'extra' money and the support offered by other family members:

> I really have nothing to spend on myself. I mean sometimes I'll ask Kevin [her husband] for a bit, if I desperately need [my hair] cut, he has paid like half of it. I think last time mum paid for half for my

birthday and Kevin paid half. But that was ages ago. ... I don't really buy myself clothes. I just manage with clothes that I've had for a long time. But it affects your self-esteem, 'cos sometimes you're wandering about and you think you look typically like a mum, you know, covered in food (laughs) ... Sometimes I go swimming. Things like that I feel bad about doing. Because of the cost, it's a fiver to go swimming. It's just a fiver that probably doesn't really exist, it should go on food.[14]

In a similar vein, Kathy Hamilton, Reader in Marketing at Strathclyde University, has highlighted how parents in low-income families attempt to protect their children from the stigma associated with poverty by purchasing branded clothing for them.[15] Whilst poor parents buying their children Diesel jeans and Nike Air Max trainers might look on the surface like irresponsible parenting, Hamilton highlights the pressure that parents feel under, and the coping strategies they employ, to ensure their children do not 'stand out' from their peers, or are excluded from social activities and opportunities as a result of their low incomes.

Value judgements about how low-income families should spend their money also have a long history, as can be seen from the chapter epigraph. In 1943, the Women's Group on Public Welfare report *Our Towns* noted, in a section called 'Wrong Spending', that:

Some hostesses of evacuated children remarked on the poor show put up by townspeople on incomes which seemed to them substantial. They found that some children who were poorly clad were nevertheless given copious pocket-money, and people who looked poverty-stricken and said that they could not afford the necessities for their children nevertheless spent freely on fares to visit them and sometimes on drink when they arrived. Others sent footwear and clothing which the countrywomen regarded as trash and a mere waste of money.[16]

Another assumption made by household poverty measures is the level of needs within households of the same size. A variety of factors, including health issues and instances of disability and age, can affect the level of income needed to achieve a decent standard of living. For example, a family where one or more of its members is experiencing poor health or has a disability may well require a higher income, all other things being equal, than households where members are relatively healthy. This may be because of such things as: higher heating bills in order to keep the house warmer; higher washing bills to reduce the possibility of infections or because of soiled clothing and bedding; higher electricity bills because of specialist medical equipment; higher transport bills if public transport is not an option because of health or mobility issues; or higher food bills where specific diets are followed.

The idea of 'the household' also plays an important symbolic role in sustaining the dominant, normative image of what a 'family' should look like. The government and other conservative commentators would have us believe that a 'stable' family is one where all members live within the same household and where resources are shared equitably. Any deviation from this single household stereotype, for any reason, is likely to be accompanied by labels such as 'dysfunctional', 'failing', 'broken' or 'troubled'. The Centre for Social Justice, for example, have ensured, in a number of its publications, that 'family breakdown', leading to lone-parent families, elides with 'social breakdown' in the national conscience.[17] In the United States there is a particular interest in the cost of 'fragile families', the moniker given to unmarried families, and the role they are perceived to play in the 'reproduction of poverty'.[18]

The durable and stable image of the household helps to mask some of the precariousness and insecurity experienced by families on low incomes. Discussions about the 'household' fail to reflect the dynamics of family life where members of the household and their relationships to others within it change, depending on a number of factors including age, relationships, health and employment. Even where members of the household remain constant, the housing situation of 'the household' may not. Talking about 'the household', which suggests a degree of safety and permanence, once again undermines discussions about the frequent house moves, spells in temporary accommodation and poor housing conditions experienced by many people living in poverty.

Recently in the UK there has also been an increase in the rhetoric surrounding those households that the government and other commentators refer to as 'workless'.[19] These are households where there is no adult in paid employment, although the description of them as 'workless' is disingenuous. Unpaid domestic work, often undertaken by women, such as child rearing, cleaning, preparing food and caring activities are discounted in this discourse, which portrays the family, and all its members, as being disengaged from any form of work. In fact, according to figures published by the Office for National Statistics in 2016, fewer than 15 per cent of 'workless households' are classed as 'unemployed'.[20] The remainder are classed as 'economically inactive' and are not usually available or expected to be available to work because of a variety of reasons such as family and caring commitments, retirement or study, or members being unable to work through sickness or disability. Labelling families as 'workless' where work is not an option for around 85 per cent of them is therefore highly misleading.

There are, then, a number of unsatisfactory assumptions made as a result of measures of poverty that remain at the household level. It must also be emphasised, that, in many cases, 'the household' does, however, reflect the living arrangements of many families and the level at which their finances are organised. Furthermore, improving on or strengthening household income statistics to reflect inter-household income dynamics should not be beyond the ability of the statisticians working on them. Unfortunately, however, the measurement of poverty at this level ensures that a number of severely marginalised groups are excluded from official poverty figures and related discussions.

EXCLUSIONS

The reliance on household surveys to gather information on poverty has implications for groups that do not neatly fit the 'household' concept and those who are likely to be missed by household surveys. For example, in July 2009 in the UK, the Child Poverty Bill was introduced to Parliament and it received royal assent on 25 March 2010, becoming the Child Poverty Act (2010). This piece of legislation transformed Tony Blair's declaration of intent to 'end child poverty forever', which he made in 1999 and saw as a '20-year mission',[21] into a legally binding commitment for the British government. The act set 'targets relating to the eradication of child poverty' but the four targets included reference only to children living in 'qualifying households'.[22] The definition of a 'qualifying household' was not provided in the act but it did require the secretary of state to ensure that the criteria are 'to have as wide an application as is reasonably practicable, having regard to the statistical surveys that are being or can reasonably be expected to be undertaken'.[23] During the scrutiny process of the Child Poverty Bill, the legislative precursor to the Child Poverty Act, the Joint Committee on Human Rights expressed concern about the potential for the 'differential treatment' of children who did not live in qualifying households, and also suggested that the government acknowledged this as a potential issue:

The Government accepts that there could be indirect discrimination because for some groups, such as Gypsy, Roma and Traveller children, and asylum seeking children, the likelihood of their being excluded is higher than for some other groups. The Government also accepts that the groups which have a lower chance of being captured by a survey include some groups which are already disadvantaged ... The beneficiaries of the duty to meet the income targets will apparently only be children in qualifying households. The legislation is therefore, on its face, designed to require policy-making to prioritise such children over others, including Roma children, children in children's home [*sic*] and asylum seeking children.[24]

The specific groups mentioned above are those that were affected by the introduction of the Child Poverty Act 2010. There are, however, other population groups, such as homeless people, adults in residential care and/or supported accommodation and those living in multi-occupancy households who are likely to be missed by many traditional household surveys. These groups are, of course, some of the poorest and most marginalised groups in society and will be at greater risk of poverty than most other sections of the population. The health economist Roy Carr-Hill, suggested in 2015 that in the UK it is also necessary to include over 100,000 service personnel in the military and around 85,000 prisoners who would also be 'missed' by household surveys.[25] He concludes that there may be as many as 1,337,000 people missing from household survey-based population estimates, with around 600,000 of those coming from the poorest quintile of the population. These figures equate to around 2 per cent of the national population, but around 4 per cent of the poorest quintile.[26]

'WORKLESS HOUSEHOLDS' AND 'TROUBLED FAMILIES'

Instead of focusing on reducing levels of poverty in the UK, or attempting to shed more light on inter-household dynamics, many sections of the Child Poverty Act were repealed in 2016 by the Conservative government, and new reporting obligations to Parliament were introduced as part of the Welfare Reform and Work Act 2016. Gone was the commitment to eradicate child poverty by 2020, and the government even removed the obligation to report annual child poverty statistics to Parliament. New obligations were introduced that ensured the number of 'workless households' and progress on 'troubled families' had to be reported to Parliament on an annual basis instead,[27] along with the educational attainment of children in England at the end of Key Stage 4 (the two years of schooling for children aged 14 to 16 that usually include GCSEs and other exams).[28]

The changes have blunt but very powerful effects. Whilst the numbers of children living in poverty have remained relatively constant in recent years and are expected to rise leading up to 2020, the numbers of children living in 'workless households' is at an all-time low, according to figures published by the Office for National Statistics in 2016.[29] Reporting the latter, but not the former, gives a distorted picture of how many children are experiencing poverty as well as what poverty really is. The latest figures, drawn from different surveys, suggest that around 2.5 million children are living in poverty, but only 193,000 children live in 'workless households'. It also masks the statistic that around 66 per cent of children living in poverty live in working households, where at least one adult is involved in paid employment of some form.[30] The pernicious and inaccurate term 'workless', which suggests a 'deficit' within the household, is also close enough to 'workshy' to help portray an image of lazy adults who are not good 'role models' for their children.

Introducing reporting requirements on the Troubled Families Programme risks making a mockery of Parliament. The official evaluation of the first phase of the programme found that it had 'no discernible impact' across a number of key areas,[31] and yet the government had already claimed that it had 'turned around' the lives of 99 per cent of the original 120,000 'troubled families' it had identified.[32] Once 'troubled families', which are referred to as 'relevant households' in the Welfare Reform and Work Act, have been 'turned around', they stay 'turned around'. With no acknowledgement that family circumstances can change, progress on the programme is always going to be positive, with increasing numbers of families deemed 'turned around'. Not only does this ignore the dynamics of poverty and people's lives more broadly, but 'turning around' 'troubled families' does not necessarily require any progress to be made in improving their financial circumstances.

In essence, the official government focus on poverty in the UK has shifted from a consideration of income that flows into the household from outside (primarily from wages and benefits) to one that is more concerned about behavioural deficits and 'problems' that allegedly originate inside the household, leading to such households being labelled 'workless' or 'troubled'. In the case of reporting on the progress of 'troubled families', the well-respected, albeit imperfect, system of measuring poverty that supports statistics concerning households below the average income have been partly marginalised in favour of a system of 'payment by results' which saw the government claim a near perfect success rate in its first phase of work with 'troubled families'. In the space of six years, we have effectively moved from a legally binding commitment to eradicate child poverty in the UK to merely reporting on how well an imaginary group of families are behaving, and how well they are doing in learning to live with their poverty and disadvantages.

DOING THE SAME AS WE'VE ALWAYS DONE

The assumptions surrounding 'the household' have implications for anti-poverty policy. We have already seen how the exclusion of certain groups from previous child poverty targets could potentially lead policymakers to focus on and prioritise children in 'qualifying households' to the detriment of other marginalised groups such as Travellers, children in care homes and asylum seekers. Other problems caused by the use of the household as the level at which poverty is measured are long-standing and go beyond simply ensuring that women and children receive a 'fair share' of household income.

A number of feminist academics have highlighted how important it is to focus on the different – and complex – gendered dimensions of poverty, rather than the simpler, gender-neutral concept of the household. Two professors of social policy, Jane Millar and Caroline Glendinning, argue that such a focus could 'lead us to explore the structural causes of women's poverty and the gendered processes in the labour market, welfare systems and domestic labour which interact to create and maintain that disadvantage'.[33] They go on to note that women, at all stages of their lives, are at greater risk of poverty than men and that their experience of poverty is likely to be more acute.[34] Women are more likely to work part time and are more likely to take periods out of the labour market for child-rearing and caring reasons. Even when they do work full time, the gender pay gap means that many women receive less pay than men doing comparable jobs. Lone parent families, most usually headed by women, are at far greater risk of poverty than households where there are two adults and where there is the potential for another wage to increase the family income. In households containing a couple, a women's ability to find employment, even where it pays poorly, can make a significant difference to the finances available to the household, and can often be the difference between having an income above instead of below the poverty line. Jan Pahl's research on the allocation of the 'whole wage' of the household highlights how, in many (but not all) low-income families, it is women who are often responsible for managing all of the household's finances, including bills, rent, clothing and food.[35] In some families, Pahl also highlights how, it was 'the man of the house' who maintained control of the family's finances. Focusing on the household, then, not only obscures the greater risk of poverty amongst women, but also obscures the causes of that poverty and the disproportionate burden placed on women when attempting to cope with or ameliorate the effect of poverty.

It is also alarming to note that recent 'reforms' to the welfare system, which were supposed to radically improve the system in the UK and help to lift thousands of people out of poverty, are based on similar assumptions about 'household income'. The coalition government's flagship reform of the welfare system was the introduction of universal credit, which was supposed to help 'simplify' the benefits system and remove the distinction between in work and out-of-work benefits.[36] It is not possible to do justice to the failings, delays and just plain cock-ups associated with universal credit here, so the focus remains on assumptions about 'household income'. Universal credit amalgamates a number of existing benefits and tax credits which are currently allocated for different reasons and purposes and may well be paid to different members of the household. In the place of many of these existing payments will be a single payment of universal credit, based on combined total earnings and household income, but made to just one adult in the household, and these payments will be paid monthly.[37] The single payment does nothing to address the issues raised above, and the monthly payment schedule makes household budgeting on a low income even more difficult, especially if control over that income is made more problematic by the single payment.

Another of the recent 'reforms' to the welfare system is the introduction of a 'benefits cap', which ensures that no 'out-of-work' household can claim more in benefits than average households earn from wages. Setting the cap at the average household wage is, firstly, disingenuous, as the benefits system acknowledges that wages are often insufficient to provide families with an adequate income and so various top-ups, in the form of tax credits and child benefit, are provided. Using the average wage level of a household, rather than the overall income of that household (including benefits, tax credits and so on) is a very political choice designed to demonstrate a 'tough' approach to poverty. Again, this 'heroic simplification' has proven very popular with certain sections of the media who appear delighted that it curbs the 'benefit lifestyles' of families receiving 'handouts' from the state.[38] When it was first introduced, the benefit cap was set at £26,000 for households headed by a couple or lone parent families with children in central London, and £23,000 for the rest of the country. In 2016, these figures were reduced respectively to £23,000 (equivalent to £442.31 per week) and £20,000 (equivalent to £384.62 per week). Although some disability-related benefits are not included in the caps, some are, and the cap takes no account of the number of children in the household or their ages. Thus, a couple with no children can receive the same level of income as a couple with one, two, three, four or more children. In the same week that it was revealed that more than 300,000 children could be pushed deeper into poverty as a result of the lowering of the benefit cap, the work and pensions secretary Dominic Green argued that it had been a 'real success' and demonstrated that the values of the government were aligned with 'those of ordinary working people', implying that households where there was no adult in work were not 'ordinary'.[39]

The shift towards classifying poverty as a product of problematic behaviour, as in the 'workless households' and 'troubled families' discourses highlighted above, also has implications for policy interventions that reputedly seek to tackle poverty. In the early days of the coalition government in 2011, Iain Duncan Smith argued against increasing the level of benefits to tackle poverty because it would only entrench 'dependency' and would, in many cases, lead to better funding for problematic behaviour.

> Take a family headed by a drug addict or someone with a gambling addiction – increase the parent's income and the chances are they will spend the money on furthering their habit, not on their children … Or take a family where no one has ever worked. Increase their benefit income – while taking no other proactive action – and you push the family further into dependency, only increasing the chance that their child will follow that same path as an adult.[40]

The introduction of 'benefit smart cards', which cannot be used for certain purchases such as tobacco or alcohol, for 'troubled families' and other families reliant on out-of-work benefits has also been mooted by the former work and pensions secretary and other politicians.[41]

MASKING COMPLEXITY?

Using 'the household' as the level at which poverty is measured can, as we have seen, be problematic and helps to mask the complexity of the lives of people living in low-income households. This situation has, however, persisted, despite the fact that some of the problems highlighted in this chapter have been known for over a hundred years, when Charles Booth and Seebohm Rowntree documented imbalances in the quality and quantity of food eaten by husbands compared to their wives and children in the early twentieth century.

There have been a number of reasons advanced as to why this situation has remained unchanged. It has been argued that feminist researchers who, interested in the ways in which gender impacts upon the experience of poverty, and vice versa, have been engaged in a 'dialogue between the deaf', with researchers interested in ascertaining the prevalence of poverty amongst the population using different methods to pursue different ends.[42] Another reason given for why we do not know more about intra-household income distribution is that the state has traditionally been reluctant to intervene in such domestic issues, although the protection of potentially vulnerable women and children is an area where the state does have a responsibility. Some people may also still believe that gender inequality within the household is not necessarily a bad thing, with the woman in the household merely playing the 'traditional' role of wife, mother and housekeeper.

Millar and Glendinning have provided a powerful case for thinking about poverty completely differently, arguing that it is not possible to just 'add on' consideration of household inequalities to existing measures of poverty. They argue that a new methodology is required to better understand poverty, one that is able to consider distinctions between 'earning, controlling, managing and consuming' an income. They suggest:

> We ... need to collect more information about how incomes enter households – who contributes what and how, and under what

conditions they obtain that income. We need to distinguish between 'direct' income (received by an individual as earnings or benefits) and 'indirect' income (received on the basis of dependency on another person). We need to distinguish between 'available' and 'non-available' income, to specify exactly who that income is available to, how much it is and what types of commodities it is intended to cover. We need to consider how, on what, and by whom income is spent and how this is related to the source of that income. All of this requires much more detailed information on the patterns of consumption within households and how these are determined.[43]

These are, of course, valid arguments if we want to understand the dynamics of poverty further. A counter argument that we know enough about poverty already can also be advanced, and it should be remembered that, until very recently, the aim of the UK government was to eradicate poverty, not to better understand its corrosive effects on different family or household members. There is a danger that arguing about the simplified notion of 'the household', which undoubtedly masks the greater risk and burden of poverty that is borne by women, distracts us from the primary goal of ending poverty. By way of example, David Cameron argued in January 2016, in a speech on improving children's life chances, that 'families are the best anti-poverty measure ever invented'.[44] He was wrong – money, in the form of a decent income, is the best anti-poverty measure ever invented.

If all families and/or households received an income that, regardless of their particular circumstances, allowed them to achieve a standard of living that was deemed acceptable by the society of which they are part, then the internal flow of that income would matter much less in many cases. Increased support from the state around issues such as school uniform, school meals, and childcare would similarly help to ensure that different members of a household did not have to make sacrifices beyond what others might view as reasonable.

Recent welfare reforms that make many poor households worse off suggest there is little appetite for change or further exploration of intra-household income distribution in political circles at the current time. This lack of concern about the impact of a reduction in the income going into many households can be contrasted with an increasing government focus on the putative behavioural failings and 'complex' or 'chaotic' lives of some poor families. As we will see in the next chapter, former prime minister David Cameron introduced the Troubled Families Programme to 'turn around' the lives of 120,000 'troubled families' in a policy development that he later argued was the 'most intensive form of state intervention there is'.[45]

7
Piles of Pringles and Crack
Behind Closed Doors

The home, if indeed it can be described as such, has usually the most striking characteristics. Nauseating odours assail one's nostrils on entry, and the source is usually located in some urine-sodden faecal-stained mattress in an upstairs room. There are no floor coverings, no decorations on the walls except perhaps the scribblings of the children and bizarre patterns formed by absent plaster. Furniture is of the most primitive, cooking utensils absent, facilities for sleeping hopeless – iron bedsteads furnished with foul mattresses and no coverings. Upstairs there is flock everywhere, which the mother assures us has come out of a mattress which she has unpacked for cleansing. But the flock seems to stay there for weeks and the cleansed and repacked mattress never appears. The bathroom is obviously the least frequented room of the building. There are sometimes faecal accumulations on the floors upstairs, and tin baths containing several days' accumulation of faeces and urine are not unknown.

R.C. Wofinden, 1944.[1]

Whilst poverty related research is often carried out in disadvantaged neighbourhoods and is usually measured at the household level, discussion of the behaviour of poor families or the conditions in which they live does not stop at the garden gate or the front door of the family home. The quotation above highlights the imagined internal geography of the homes of 'problem families' in the 1940s. It should be noted that this description did not describe a particular house that had been visited by R.C. Wofinden, a medical officer in Bristol. According to Wofinden, it depicted a typical 'problem family' house. The social historian John Welshman has noted that whilst it was a misleading portrayal of the conditions of many poor families in the 1940s, it proved to be a very powerful image and one that was widely quoted at the time.[2] In the 1960s, and in discussing concerns about poor people allegedly enjoying themselves too much (implicitly at 'our' expense), the sociologist William Ryan provided a good summary of some of middle-class concerns about the home lives and activities of their poorer peers:

> We complain about the sex lives of the poor in much the same way we complain about their having television sets. We no longer require of the poor that they starve to death on the streets, but we do believe that it's good for them to be a little hungry. We certainly won't stand for them enjoying their life in any way at all, else what would motivate them to overcome their somewhat shameful state of poverty?[3]

Concerns about sexual activity, television sets, food consumption and leisure activities have continued to the present day, with numerous negative images circulating about what goes on 'behind closed doors' of poor families. This chapter examines some of the imagined internal spaces of poor families. The liminal space of the front door, symbolically as well as physically important as the threshold between the public external space outside the home and the private internal universe of the family is discussed, along with other rooms that are often deployed, implicitly or explicitly, in poverty discourses. The image of the front room of the low-income family, replete with its seemingly obligatory flat-screen television, empty takeaway boxes and 'sofa of despair' is expounded before attention turns to the 'absent present' of the kitchen. The kitchen itself is rarely discussed, but the food practices – the storage, preparation and consumption of food – within the home is a key way of Othering people living on low incomes. The idea that kitchens are largely redundant spaces in poor families' homes, or used in non-traditional ways, is another way of signifying a heavily gendered difference and distinction between 'the poor' and 'the non-poor'. The last space discussed is the bedroom, which, like the kitchen, is not always discussed explicitly. The bedtime routines and activities of poor families are, however, key components of debates about the domestic competence of women in poor households. The chapter concludes with a discussion highlighting how the heavily gendered focus on the domestic micro-practices of poor families deflects attention away from wider structural, environmental and public issues that structure those practices.

Not all spaces of the family home are discussed here. Space precludes a discussion of 'the bathroom' and the associated issues of dirt and hygiene that circulate around poor families. This issue has been written about extensively elsewhere, from different theoretical positions, and it is difficult to summarise this more adroitly than George Orwell did when he stated that 'that's what we were taught – the lower classes smell'.[4] Similarly, the gardens of poorer or working-class families are not discussed here, although as we noted in discussions about 'street-oriented' families in Chapter 5, the cleanliness and upkeep of gardens and yards is but one way better off citizens judge the morals and values of many poorer, or working-class, families.

THE FRONT DOOR: CROSSING THE THRESHOLD

Just as the street corner is an important symbolic space, so too is the front door of a family home. The door, and even the doorstep, is an important threshold, marking the boundary where the public arena ends and the private, intimate space of the family home begins. Despite the spaces and rooms behind the front door traditionally being seen as the separate universe of 'the family', the state has a long history of intervening in this realm. Professionals, such as housing officers or the police, are required to undertake home visits from time to time, but there are also a number of other professions where home visit forms a core part of their work.[5] Invariably, in these situations, the threshold of the front door is portrayed as a risky, dangerous, liminal space where confrontations are likely.

The Troubled Families Programme, set up in the aftermath of the 2011 riots, and now in its second phase, is based on a 'family intervention' model that prioritises a single 'dedicated' keyworker working intensively with families, often in their own home.[6] The ability of the worker to develop a strong relationship based on trust with the family is central to this model. Louise Casey, the senior civil servant originally in charge of the programme, has articulated, on a number of occasions, what it was that made the 'family intervention' approach different.[7] In 2012, in a speech given to Troubled Families coordinators working in local authorities, she argued that 'we have to be bold about getting past [troubled families'] front doors'.[8] The following year, she told the Communities and Local Government Select Committee, which was conducting an inquiry into the progress of the programme and similar schemes, that:

> we have staff and workers who are extraordinary. They walk into these families' lives; they do not invite them to an office for an appointment with a letter. They walk through the front door and into the front

room past two extraordinarily difficult and dangerous-looking dogs that they hope are locked in the kitchen. They have to sit on a settee, often in a pretty rough environment with some very aggressive people, and, with kids not in school and people all over the criminal justice system and so on.[9]

Casey sought to portray the family workers involved in the programme as dynamic and courageous, and thus different from the stereotypical 'pen-pushing' bureaucrat who would sit passively in an office in a town hall rather than taking the initiative. Whilst many local authorities have sought to recontextualise central government messages about 'troubled families',[10] some local authorities, and the workers they employ, obviously believe in the importance of being able to cross the symbolic threshold of the front door. One local authority published a quote from one of its male key workers in a bulletin promoting its achievements in the first year of the programme:

> When mum was finding it hard to manage her mental health I would often have to leave a whole morning or afternoon to visit as it has sometimes taken over an hour of banging on the door to get in to the house. Persistence has got me in the door even on bad days.[11]

Quite how or why a male agent of the state thinks it is 'good practice' to be 'banging on the door' of a vulnerable woman with mental health issues for over an hour is not expanded on in the bulletin. These quotes, however, highlight precisely what the French anthropologist Celine Rosselin, drawing on other anthropologists' work, has described as 'the dangerous act of crossing the threshold'.[12] She argues that crossing thresholds marks a 'beginning of new statuses' that are often controlled by ritual. Thus, we see workers of the state, traditionally mocked for being boring, lazy and inefficient, transformed into 'persistent, assertive and challenging' workers set apart from their colleague by virtue of their dynamism and bravery.[13]

The act of crossing the threshold of the front door has other powerful symbolic properties. It locates the source of the problems faced, or caused, by 'troubled families' within the home itself and, as the quotes also demonstrate, often as the result of maternal failings. The private domestic sphere of the family home is still associated with the work of mothers. Whilst men traditionally went out to work, mothers would be involved in the domestic labour of, for example, keeping the house clean, getting children ready for school and preparing food. When the government initiate a programme that emphasises the need for workers to get in through the front door and help families with domestic tasks, the implication that disadvantaged working-class mothers are failing is clear for all to see. If anyone was in any doubt, Casey has also stated that, 'This is all about making sure the mum is in control of her household'.[14]

'SOFAS OF DESPAIR' AND FLAT-SCREEN TVS

The imagined front rooms of people living in poverty are also important symbolic spaces that are often used to portray their deviancy or difference from the 'rest of us'. The British sitcom *The Royle Family*, which depicted the minutiae of working-class family life, was shot almost entirely in the front room of the family home. Family members, partners and friends would sit in the same armchair or place on the sofa and conversations would take place with the television on in the background. The British sociologist Bev Skeggs has highlighted how the programme, intended to represent an ironic commentary of working-class stereotypes, including their immobility, offers a 'potential "truth" to middle-class viewers in the absence of any other alternative perspectives'.[15]

The portrayal of working class families staying indoors, chained to their sofas, watching endless amounts of television on large flat-screen TVs is therefore a powerful one. It locates them as not being where they should be – 'at work' or 'in school'. People 'sitting at home on benefits',[16] as David Cameron once put it, are portrayed as not engaging in productive behaviour of any sort, an image compounded by the pernicious term 'workless families'. The journalist and novelist Clare Allan has summarised the way in which the government have created a 'them and us' situation – a 'vision of divisions'[17] to use Bourdieu's words – comprising a 'them' of 'workless families' and their reliance on benefits, and an 'us' of 'hardworking families' paying for 'them':

> the workshy family living in their taxpayer-funded paradise, sitting on their sofa eating Domino's pizza, watching satellite TV, and laughing out loud at mugs like you, slaving for 60 hours a week, with a three-hour-a-day commute on top, because you can't afford to live anywhere near work, who are paying for the whole shebang.[18]

Eric Pickles, a former government minister, has described the work of the Troubled Families Programme as being about 'getting [troubled families] off the sofa of despair',[19] whilst Louise Casey, as highlighted earlier, has suggested that the approach involves family workers sitting on settees, and that, 'It's OK for us to say that we should have aspirations for these families beyond a life spent on the settee.'[20]

In the United States, the American equivalent of 'the sofa of despair' and its inhabitant, the 'couch potato', is someone who 'sits on the couch eating bon bons'. The expression manages to incorporate assumptions about poor dietary habits into the depiction of lazy working-class people. In discussing a Big Society tinged forerunner of the Troubled Families Programme, one that would see volunteer 'family champions' working with 'workless families', the *Guardian* columnist Tanya Gold suggested that it 'conjures the image of workshy beasts lying in piles of Pringles and crack, waiting to be shouted at by Hyacinth Bucket'.[21]

Images of families eating unhealthy take-out meals in front of the television similarly manage to combine two types of problematic behaviour when associated with low-income families. Jamie Oliver, the celebrity chef who has campaigned for better quality school meals has argued that 'modern-day poverty' isn't quite as hard as it should be:

I'm not judgmental, but I've spent a lot of time in poor communities, and I find it quite hard to talk about modern-day poverty. You might remember that scene in *Ministry Of Food* [one of Oliver's television shows], with the mum and the kid eating chips and cheese out of Styrofoam containers, and behind them is a massive fucking TV. It just didn't weigh up.[22]

Plenty of people who take the time to respond to online news articles or comment pieces on poverty appear to share Oliver's definition of what constitutes poverty. No doubt, as the broadcaster and journalist Andrew Collins has noted, their views are influenced by the amount of time 'reality' TV-show cameras spend showing the TVs of people living in poverty:

If there's one thing we know about the poor – other than, as Jesus spotted, they will always be with us – it's that they all own huge flatscreen TVs. If anything unites the feckless benefit scrounger of Tory nightmares, the determined jobseeker of Tory dreams and the blameless widowed pensioner counting the days before being packed off to 'a home', it's a 32 in. plasma. We know this because prying TV cameras are never out of their social housing. I sincerely hope these often blameless victims of a global downturn engineered by a financial sector they didn't vote for don't actually watch the documentaries and reality shows they help to make. They'd be forgiven for kicking in the screen.[23]

The sofa, the flat-screen televisions and the empty takeaway boxes, Styrofoam containers or snacks are all important symbols because they help to locate leisure time and activities of people living in poverty within the home. The political portrayal of the fixity of their physical location neatly symbolises the alleged lumpen nature of their social deprivation and marginalisation.

Whilst middle-class families are engaged in consuming culture in the public domain, at restaurants, theatres, cinemas, cafés, sports events and the like, their working class Others are chained to their front room, lacking both the economic capital to access such opportunities and the cultural capital to appreciate them. When young members of poor or 'troubled families' do venture outside, they are portrayed as 'rampaging around the neighbourhood',[24] causing misery to everyone; and when they remain indoors they are depicted as largely staying at home, leading deprived and uncultured lives, unable to belong to wider social and cultural networks because of their anti-social behaviour and lifestyle. Their fixity, their lack of mobility and the 'limited' forms of culture they are satisfied with are thus utilised as a symbolic marker that can be used to demonstrate that 'the poor' are 'different' in key aspects from their more mobile, selective middle-class and 'non-poor' Others.

THE KITCHEN: JUDGING MUMS

The imagery of poor families eating takeaway food in front of the television is part of a wider narrative about the alleged poor dietary choices and lack of culinary skills amongst working-class families. Although the kitchen is rarely mentioned or discussed explicitly, the issue of food – quality, quantity, preparation and consumption – is often invoked in emphasising the ways in which people living in poverty are different to those who are not. The kitchen, then, is imagined as an absent present, a place where working-class families do not store, prepare or consume food. The suggestion by Louise Casey that the kitchen is where 'dangerous looking dogs' are locked up in the houses of 'troubled families' cleverly plays on fears about danger, deviancy and dirt.

The narrative about poor eating habits, like most other narratives about the alleged failings of the working classes, is one with a long history. In his book *The Road to Wigan Pier*, an account of working-class life in the north of England during the 1930s, George Orwell recounts the story of a Communist Party member on the issue:

> In London, he said, parties of Society dames now have the cheek to walk into East End houses and give shopping lessons to the wives of the unemployed. He gave this as an example of the mentality of the governing class. First you condemn a family to live on thirty shillings a week, and then you have the damned impertinence to tell them how they are to spend their money.[25]

In the report the Women's Group on Public Welfare wrote just a few years later, there is a long section on 'bad eating habits', which sets out how 'different' the eating customs of the poor children evacuated from the slums were in comparison to those of their rural middle-class hostesses. The report states that the 'hostesses' 'tended to attribute all the oddities in the children's dietetic habits to poverty or maternal laziness, ignorance and neglect'.[26] The report then goes on to highlight the constraints that poverty inflicts on the eating habits of families, many of which still ring true today, including the prohibitive cost of healthier food, an income insufficient to purchase enough food of any quality, and a home environment which might not be conducive to everyone sitting down to an evening meal together.

Some families will not have the funds to afford a dining table and chairs, or to replace ones that get broken. Many family homes will have small kitchens and no dining room, meaning meals in front of the television become more of a practical decision than a lifestyle choice. Parents and children may eat at different times due to working patterns and other time pressures. As was discussed in the previous chapter, one reason that mothers may not sit and eat breakfast or evening meals with their children is because they do not always eat those meals due to not being able to afford to feed all the members of the household all of the time.

Takeaway food or 'ready meals' often have the advantage of high calorific content for their cost. On a low income, it is, quite simply, easier to ensure people get the calories they need and ensure they feel 'full up' by providing them with high-calorie foods than it is by attempting to feed them, for example, vegetable crudités, quinoa and salad. Similarly, when feeding people on a low budget, it is important to ensure that food is not wasted. Attempting to feed children new, often healthy, options is not, as any parent will testify, an easy job, and if there is only one option in the cupboard or the fridge, parents needs to be confident that their children will eat it. Jamie Oliver's observation that Sicilian street cleaners can 'knock out the most amazing pasta' using 25 mussels, 10 cherry tomatoes, and a packet of spaghetti for 60 pence matters little if a child refuses to eat it.[27] Jack Monroe, a writer who has campaigned around issues of food poverty, having had personal experience of it, has likened Oliver to a 'poverty tourist', bringing to mind the slummers of Victorian times, and has written a compelling account of what life on a low-income can mean for parents of young children. Monroe suggested Oliver 'try it':

> For a month, or two, or five. Unscrew your lightbulbs, turn off your fridge, sell anything you can see lying around that you might get more than £2 for. Missing days of meals, with the heating off all winter, selling your son's shoes and drinking his formula milk that the food bank gave you. Stop going out. Walk everywhere, even in the pouring rain, in your only pair of shoes, with a wet and sobbing three-year-old. Drag that three-year-old into every pub and shop in unreasonable walking distance and ask if they have any job vacancies. Get home, soaking, still unemployed, to dry out in a freezing cold flat. Then drag yourself to the cooker to pour some pasta into a pan, pour some chopped tomatoes on top, and try not to hurl it across the room when your son tells you that he doesn't like it. You're full of rain and heartache and anger and despair and it's starting to seep through the cracks. This person does not pop down to a local market and smile sweetly at the stallholder for a handful of gourmet vegetables. This person throws whatever is in the cupboard into a saucepan and prays that her child will eat it.[28]

The complexity of attempting to provide a balanced healthy diet for a family on a low income is therefore lost on the likes of Jamie Oliver, who has suggested that the contents of some packed lunch boxes are akin to child abuse,[29] and has also been forthright about parents giving their children sugary snacks:

I've spent two years being PC about parents. It's kind of time to say if you're giving very young kids bottles and bottles of fizzy drink you're a fucking arsehole, you're a tosser. If you've giving bags of shitty sweets at that very young age, you're an idiot.[30]

Meanwhile, the *Daily Telegraph* columnist Theodor Dalrymple has suggested that the lack of structured feeding routines in poor households and the lack of shared mealtimes, often in households that, in his words, lack a 'normal family structure', has meant that 'children became foragers or hunter-gatherers in their own homes, going to the fridge whenever they felt like it and grazing on prepared foods'.[31] In an article arguing that it was bad eating habits and not poverty that caused obesity, Dalrymple agreed that the availability of fresh produce in many poor neighbourhoods was often limited, but also rhetorically asked, 'if heroin can reach these areas (and it can), surely the humble lettuce can do so?'. He went on to provide an anecdote to encapsulate his argument:

I happen to be staying at the moment in a provincial English town. Often in its centre I observe two fat mothers side by side pushing their almost equally fat infants in pushchairs grazing on milk chocolate hippopotami or cheeseburger-flavoured potato rings (it is never too soon to learn). These perpetual snacks have the great advantage of keeping the nippers quiet while their mothers discuss the shortcomings of their respective boyfriends; unfortunately, they are harmful for longer-term and more important objectives.[32]

The intense gaze on the eating habits of poor families – what they eat, how much they pay for it, where they eat it and so on – ensures that little attention is paid to wider factors that influence all of these issues. A strong contemporary policy focus on 'nudging' people towards healthier lifestyle choices leaves little room for discussion of the constraints on their choices, or about the flaccid attempts to regulate the behaviour of multinational corporations. The UK government's child obesity strategy, launched in 2016, was described as 'embarrassing' by public health experts, partly as a result of the removal of proposed attempts to restrict the advertising of junk food and restricting promotional offers on unhealthy food in supermarkets.[33] The behaviour of large food manufacturers, in relation to their intense lobbying of government and funding of supportive research, has been likened to the behaviour of tobacco companies who, in years gone by, attempted to convince politicians and the public that smoking was not harmful.[34] In discussions about food and poverty, however, the (mal)practices of large companies receive relatively little condemnation in comparison with the imagined culinary shortcomings of marginalised mothers.

THE BEDROOM: 'FEARFUL PLACES'

There is also a long history to middle-class concerns about the bedrooms of low income families, and the deviancy and indiscipline associated with them. George Orwell remarked, in *The Road to Wigan Pier*, that 'it is in the rooms upstairs that the gauntness of poverty really discloses itself', and that 'many of the bedrooms I saw were fearful places'.[35] The nearly contemporaneous report of the Women's Group on Public Welfare included a section on 'bad sleeping habits', which noted that the 'unsatisfactory type of evacuated mother … not only went to bed very late but lay abed until all hours in the morning and sometimes until high noon, regardless of whether there were children to be washed and fed or not'.[36]

Working-class women have also traditionally been portrayed as sexually promiscuous and 'deviant', in different ways, on both sides of the Atlantic, especially in recent years. The sociologist William Ryan wrote, tongue-in-cheek, about 'the prevalence of bastards' in 1971,[37] and Charles Murray, the 'unemployed political scientist of mediocre repute'[38] who did much to propagate the idea of an underclass in the 1980s, was concerned about illegitimacy 'sky-rocketing'.[39] Large families, inter-racial relationships, teenage motherhood and the alleged existence of 'men deserts' in the UK have also attracted public disapproval in recent times.

In the 1970s, the concept of the 'welfare queen' gained notoriety, helped in large part by newspaper and magazine articles, and a number of speeches by Ronald Reagan, who was at that time governor of California. Linda Taylor, a career criminal who was alleged to have been involved in assaults, thefts, kidnappings and murders, as well as welfare fraud, was arguably the first 'welfare queen'. Taylor came to national attention when Reagan based a section of a speech on her behaviour, focusing on her activities in relation to fraud rather than her other alleged crimes. Reagan stated that she had operated in 14 states using 127 names, claimed to be the mother of 14 children, was using 50 addresses in Chicago alone, had posed as an open-heart surgeon and owned 'three new cars [and] a full-length mink coat'.[40]

Taylor's story was so extreme that it was not necessary for Reagan to exaggerate many aspects of it. However, as time progressed, the concept of the 'welfare queen' began to be used to describe a wider group of women who were not enjoying the proceeds of crime in the same way that Taylor was. In an examination of the origins of the 'welfare queen' narrative, the historian Julilly Kohler-Hausmann has suggested that

> While the original welfare queens were outliers even within the scope of typical welfare fraud cases, the moniker in time worked to suggest that 'average' AFDC [Aid to Families with Dependent Children] recipients were lazy, sexually promiscuous (typically African American) women who shirk both domestic and wage labour.[41]

The term 'welfare queen' came to be shorthand for African American women who received financial support from the state for raising their children. These women were stereotypically portrayed as having numerous children out of wedlock in order to maximise possible income from the state. The concept was heavily racialised and came to be synonymous with ideas about a growing black urban 'underclass' in the 1980s, and was used as evidence for subsequent attempts to constrain the cost of welfare in the United States.

The concept of the 'teenage mother' has been deployed to similar effect in the UK in recent years. The discourse surrounding young parents often attempts to portray young working-class women as desperate to get pregnant in order to be 'given' a house or flat of their own. In 1992, the then secretary of state for social security, Peter Lilley, read out a 'little list' of people he was 'rooting out' as scroungers. The list, based on a song from a Gilbert and Sullivan comic opera, included the following lines: 'There's young ladies who get pregnant just to jump the housing queue, / And dads who won't support the kids of ladies they have ... kissed'.[42]

The sociologist Imogen Tyler has written powerfully about the popular imagery often associated with contemporary working-class mothers – sometimes referred to as a 'chav mum' who is, at the current time, 'the quintessential sexually excessive, single mother: an immoral, filthy, ignorant, vulgar, tasteless, working-class whore'.[43] Tyler skilfully highlights that this image of the promiscuous and poor Other, with her 'gaggle of mixed race children', also says a lot about the portrayal of middle-class women:

> For whilst the chav mum represents a highly undesirable reproductive body, this figure can also be read as symptomatic of an explosion of anxiety about dropping fertility rates amongst the white middle classes. Indeed, the disgust for and fascinated obsession with the chav mum's 'easy fertility' is bound up with a set of social angst about infertility amongst middle-class women, a group continually chastised for 'putting career over motherhood' and 'leaving it too late' to have children. The figure of the chav mum not only mocks poor white teenage mothers but also challenges middle-class women to face their 'reproductive responsibilities'.[44]

In contemporary policy discourses, the children in 'troubled families' are assumed to lack, for example, bedtime routines, and teenagers are often portrayed as spending long periods of time in their bedroom. Meanwhile, the mothers in 'troubled families' are often portrayed as spending long periods of time in bed, and thus neglecting their domestic responsibilities.[45]

We can see then that it is not always necessary to invoke images of 'the bedroom' explicitly. In middle-class homes, bedrooms are purported to be places of rest and tranquillity and recovery. In the homes of the Othered working classes, bedrooms are places of deviancy, difference and debauchery. Poor children, we are led to believe, do not go to bed at a set time, or they spend too much time in bed. Their mothers, when their time in bed is discussed, are portrayed as being overly active in the bedroom, with a corresponding inactivity in relation to domestic chores. Once again, the focus on putative behaviour deflects attention away from possible causes of these alleged failings. Overcrowding means that many children in low-income households may be forced to share bedrooms with siblings, sometimes of the opposite sex. Some children or parents will sleep in living areas downstairs due to a lack of sufficient and appropriate bedrooms, an issue that will only increase as a result of the UK government's bedroom tax. Children may experience disturbed sleeping patterns due to housing issues or health problems. Parents may well spend time in bed, or with a duvet on the sofa in order to keep warm if they are unable to heat their home adequately, but these reasons rarely form part of dominant discourses about people living in poverty.

DISCUSSION

The intimate, private, domestic and, most importantly, the phantasmic spaces of the family home, rarely seen by members of the middle classes outside the confines of poverty porn television programmes, are often used to highlight the alleged difference between 'them' and 'us'. Many people will never understand the domestic lives of Others given that narratives and images are often mediated and represented through television programmes and politicians' statements. Bourdieu's contention then, that the truth of any interaction can never be found at the site of that interaction, seems particularly relevant in discussing the conditions and activities associated with poor families in their own homes. The lives of 'troubled families', many of them experiencing long-term health issues, disability or limiting illness, cannot be 'turned around' by an assertive worker exhorting them to get off their backsides and into work. The food 'choices' of low-income families, whatever they are, cannot be adequately explained away as the uninformed work of 'tossers' and 'arseholes' as Jamie Oliver has suggested. And the depiction of working-class women as over-sexualised and 'rough and ready' in the bedroom needs to be simply dismissed as the outpourings of middle-class masculine fantasies or feminine fears.

These household spaces are literally 'behind closed doors'. They are thus very much imagined geographies, ones which, if most members of the public are ever to see them, require representation. These spaces are symbolically very powerful, and ones which are also heavily gendered. The family home, or the domestic sphere more generally, is still associated with women, and narratives about domestic deviance and difference perpetuate imagined deficiencies of working-class women. Such a perspective again ignores the structural factors and political decisions, usually taken by men, that affect the domestic lives of poor families, and which constrain the abilities of their members to live the kinds of lives and take part in the social and cultural activities that many people take for granted and assume to be 'normal'. A focus on the alleged shortcomings of working-class women, usually mothers, also fails to acknowledge the skills, perseverance and resilience of these women in ensuring that many people experiencing poverty, especially children, are shielded from its full effects. This situation is as relevant today as it was over a hundred years ago when Eleanor Rathbone, an MP, philanthropist and campaigner for women's rights, noted in a report on the condition of widows under the Poor Law in Liverpool at the turn of the twentieth century:

> It is hard for a woman to be an efficient housewife and parent while she is living under conditions of extreme penury – obliged to live in an insanitary house because it is cheap; waging a continual war with the vermin which infests such houses; unable to spend anything on repairs and replacements of household gear unless she takes it off the weekly food money; limited in the use of soap, soda and even hot water, because of the cost of coal; with no pennies to spare for the postage or tram rides that would keep up her own or her children's intercourse with relatives at a distance, or give them a day's holiday in the parks or on the sands, or enable her to frequent the Labour Exchange to seek better work for herself and the elder boys and girls; and trying through it all to earn part of the family income as well as to administer it. The astonishing thing to us is not that so many women fail to grapple with the problem successfully, but that any succeed.[46]

8

Less Public, More Private

The Shifting Spaces of the State

[B]rick by brick, edifice by edifice, we are slowly dismantling the big-state structures.

David Cameron, 2012.[1]

This chapter turns its attention to the spaces of the state, the concrete settings in which the state engages with poor and marginalised individuals, families and communities. The changing nature of welfare states has been well documented, with the geographer Jamie Peck, amongst many others, highlighting the expansion of workfare activities across the globe in recent times.[2] Peck defines the 'essence of workfarism' as involving 'the imposition of a range of compulsory programs and mandatory requirements for welfare recipients with a view to *enforcing work while residualizing welfare*.[3] This ideological shift has seen the reduction of broadly supportive welfare policies at the same time that workfare programmes that increase conditionality within the welfare system and attempt to implement 'activation policies' to get people into work of any sort have been rolled out. Originating in the United States in the 1980s, workfare policies can now be found across the globe, and successive UK governments have embraced the principle that with the rights enjoyed by citizens come responsibilities to be engaged in employment-related activity.

The physical and spatial shifts of the state in recent times have received relatively less attention, despite the fact that welfare reforms, cuts to public services and structural changes to the state have affected where the state operates from and where it engages with citizens. In the UK, the impact of the government's post-2010 welfare reforms has fallen unevenly across the country, hitting the poorest areas hardest. Public buildings such as youth clubs, children's centres, housing offices and libraries have closed, reduced their opening hours or been transferred to voluntary sector or private sector companies as a result of cuts to local authority services. At the same time, and as we began to see in the last chapter, the desire to intervene in the homes and domestic practices of marginalised families has increased. The rhetorical focus on these private spaces and the primacy of the relationship forged between keyworker and members of 'troubled' families deflects attention away not only from structural factors, but also the monitoring and regulating of families that takes place virtually, in 'the cloud', as a result of largely unreported data collection, sharing and analysis.

HITTING THE POOREST PLACES HARDEST

After the 2010 general election, both parties in the coalition government stated that, at a time of unprecedented economic uncertainty, it was necessary to put party differences aside and govern 'in the national interest'.[4] Governing in the national interest turned out to mean initiating a range of punitive structural and welfare reforms, which changed the shape of the state dramatically in the UK. Concepts such as the 'Big Society', which was aimed at getting volunteers to step in and replace services previously provided and funded by the state, and the expansion of private sector involvement in education and health spheres helped to fundamentally change how public services were delivered. Severe cuts were imposed on local government spending and a top-down reorganisation of the NHS was undertaken, whilst the government paradoxically also espoused the virtues of localism and decentralisation.

At the same time, the UK government launched a programme of welfare reforms and cuts to services that placed 'the welfare state ... under the most severe and sustained attack it has faced'.[5] Perhaps the most comprehensive analysis of the welfare reforms introduced since 2010 comes from two reports published by the economic geographers Christina Beatty and Steve Fothergill.[6] They state that the cumulative loss to households as a result of the government's welfare reforms since 2010 will be £27 billion per year by 2020/21.[7] In setting out the uneven impact of these reforms, they argue that, 'as a general rule, the more deprived the local authority the greater the financial loss', and they highlight that '83 per cent of the loss from the post-2015 reforms ... can be expected to fall on families with dependent children', with losses to lone parents with two or more children estimated to be, on average, £1,750 per year.[8] Pensioner couples, by contrast, are expected to lose only around £40 per annum on average and couples with no children will lose an estimated £200 per annum by the same date.[9]

Welfare reforms introduced since 2010 have thus had disproportionate impacts on poor families with children, with lone parents, usually women, particularly badly hit. Many reforms affect individuals and families directly, but some reforms such as those which affect council tax and housing benefit also potentially affect the revenue streams of local services, with the hardest hit areas being those with large numbers of poor and disadvantaged families. The simultaneous withdrawal of local government funding linked to deprivation has also resulted in the most disadvantaged areas of the UK being most affected by cuts to local government services.[10] In an examination of the effects of government spending cuts on local authorities, researchers have noted that local government has 'suffered a faster rate of cuts than most other areas of government spending', with a '27 per cent reduction in the spending power of the sector in England between 2010/11 and 2014/15'.[11]

Mirroring the uneven impact of the welfare reforms highlighted above, researchers at the Institute for Fiscal Studies, a think tank, note that 'spending cuts were highest in areas where spending was initially highest – London, followed by the North East and North West – and generally lower in regions where spending was initially lower'.[12] The areas that saw the largest cuts, then, were the areas that had previously been identified as being comparatively poorer areas and having higher local needs.

The cuts to local services have resulted in neighbourhood-based public facilities closing, reducing their opening hours or restricting access to certain groups. In 2015, it was estimated that more than 1,000 Sure Start children's centres aimed at pre-school children and their parents had either closed or had had their services so seriously curtailed that they could no longer be properly called a children's centre and had been 'de-registered' since the 2010 general election.[13] Many youth clubs and youth centres have faced similar situations, and national campaigns have been organised to save public libraries from closure, often without success.[14] Leisure centres and sports facilities have been handed over to private 'trusts' in order to keep them open.[15] Few providers of social housing in the UK retain neighbourhood housing offices anymore and, where they do, tenants and residents are often not free to 'drop in' and speak to a worker, with pre-booked appointments systems increasingly becoming the norm. In May 2015, Manchester City Council banned homeless people from using their toilets following the setting up of a protest camp outside the library.[16] Added to the withdrawal or scaling back of many services from local neighbourhoods, central and local government departments appear increasingly keen to engage with citizens even more remotely still, through increased use of call centres and new services and welfare-related programmes sometimes being introduced on a 'digital-by-default' basis.

One particularly good example of the way that structural changes to the state can impact on service delivery can be found in the proposal by Sodexo – a private sector firm involved in, among other activities, the partial privatisation of the probation service – to replace face-to-face meetings with biometric kiosks. In early 2015, around 70 per cent of the probation service was privatised, in a move that the then justice secretary Chris Grayling saw as 'the best of the private and voluntary sectors, working together with the public sector, to cut reoffending'.[17] In March 2015, the *Guardian* reported that Sodexo, the largest private probation contractor in the UK, planned to 'allow offenders to report in at ATM-style electronic kiosks' and introduce supervision meetings via call centres for some people on probation. The machines, which would use biometric, finger-print technology to recognise offenders, would replace around 700 members of staff.[18]

Drawing on case studies in four areas, the authors of a report called *The Cost of the Cuts*, commissioned by the Joseph Rowntree Foundation, demonstrate that local authorities have attempted to protect front-line services but that this has not always been possible and, even where it has, these services have not always emerged unscathed.[19] The authors also note that 'small "savings" can make a big difference to poorer individuals',[20] arguing that a change in opening hours, or changing the day of a service or location of a session, can affect people without the resources or flexibility to adapt to or accommodate such changes. Participants in their research also expressed concern about the impact of the cuts on their neighbourhood, with one participant suggesting that their local area had been 'abandoned' by the council.[21]

FROM THE STREET TO THE FRONT DOOR

The front-line workers who are tasked with delivering public services are often referred to as 'street-level bureaucrats'. Michael Lipsky, an American public policy academic, coined the term in the 1970s and it crossed over into mainstream usage when he published a book on the subject in 1980 called *Street-Level Bureaucrats: Dilemmas of the Individuals in Public Service*.[22]

Lipsky argued that members of the public experienced government policies through the actions of individuals with whom they had interactions. It was, for example, through the actions and decisions of housing officers and tenancy support officers that government housing policy would be experienced, through interactions with social workers that social care or child protection strategies would be experienced, and through interactions and relations with classroom teachers that education policies would be experienced. Government policies are often blunt tools that require adaptation and revision in order to make them work in practice. Street-level workers, then, often have to negotiate, adapt, subvert and sometimes resist different aspects of the policies that shape their daily work. Lipsky's argument therefore, was that it was these street-level public officials who were the real policy makers; they were the ones who decided how individuals or families received and experienced public programmes.

The focus on 'street-level' interactions between state workers and citizens reflects a particular view of the spaces in which encounters between citizens and low-level bureaucrats generally take place. It also appears to mirror the view of 'the street' amongst American urban sociologists as the place where residents of poor neighbourhoods could be found 'hanging out'. The 'neighbourhood' has also often been a key site where the state has attempted to assert control over marginalised populations through various neighbourhood- or area-based interventions, such as regeneration schemes similar to those discussed earlier and projects like neighbourhood policing teams, neighbourhood wardens and the establishment of and support for neighbourhood watch programmes.

Lipsky notes that the 'concrete settings' for encounters between the state and its citizens are often in public spaces or public buildings. Jobcentres, health centres, schools, housing offices, police stations, libraries, children's centres, parks and streets are all (more or less) public spaces where members of the public encounter public sector workers, as well as other members of the public with whom they may share common interests and concerns. It is likely, for example, that the majority of people entering a jobcentre or a welfare office will be looking for work or enquiring about support in relation to their (un)employment. Similarly, most parents at a school will have some concerns in common relating to the education of their children. Lipsky argues that public buildings represent a 'visible, accessible and blameable collective target' when there are grievances against public services or officials.[23] Grass-roots campaigns against the closure or reduction of public services, or particular aspects of them, often target town halls, civic centres or local buildings. Lipsky draws on earlier work by Frances Fox Piven and Richard Cloward, which highlights how everyday interactions and experience frame people's perceptions of what needs to change in order for their situation to improve:

> [P]eople experience deprivation and oppression within a concrete setting, not as the end product of large and abstract processes and it is the concrete experience that molds their discontent into specific grievances against specific targets. Workers experience the factory, the speeding rhythm of the assembly line, the foreman, the spies and the guards, the owner and the paycheck. They do not experience monopoly capitalism. People on relief experience the shabby waiting rooms, the overseer or the caseworker, and the dole. They do not experience American social welfare policy. Tenants experience the leaking ceilings and cold radiators, and they recognize the landlord. They do not realise the banking, real estate and construction systems. No small wonder, therefore, that when the poor rebel, they so often rebel against the overseer of the poor, or the slumlord or the middling merchant, and not against the banks or the governing elites to whom the overseer, the slumlord, and the merchant also defer. In other words, it is the daily experience of people that shapes their grievances, establishes the measure of their demands, and points out the targets of their anger.[24]

The closure of many of these public buildings, or the reduced access they offer, are not the only form of withdrawal from the spaces where the state has traditionally operated. Welfare reforms such as the 'bedroom tax', which punishes people living in social housing for having a putatively 'spare' bedroom, and the benefits cap have meant that many people on low incomes and reliant on some form of state support have had to move home. In the first wave of welfare reforms, the benefit cap mainly affected families in London. The then mayor of London, Boris Johnson, stated in 2012 that he would not tolerate the 'Kosovo-style

'social cleansing' of poor families in London when reports surfaced of
London boroughs looking to places such as Nottingham, Stoke and
Derby to rehouse families affected by the welfare reforms.[25] The Focus
E15 campaign in Newham, London, sprung up when a group of young
mothers were served with eviction notices after Newham Council cut
its funding to a hostel for young homeless people, and told that if they
wanted rehousing they would be forced to move into private rented
accommodation as far away as Manchester, Hastings and Birmingham.
The mothers and their supporters have demanded 'social housing, not
social cleansing' and campaigned for bringing empty homes on the
Carpenter's Estate in Newham back into use with the twin slogans 'These
people need homes' and 'These homes need people'.[26]

In 2015, it was calculated that nearly 50,000 poor families had been
moved from their local authority area since 2010, mainly from central
London to greater London, effectively leaving behind many social and
family networks and schools and potentially making travel to work
more difficult.[27] Nearly 3,000 of these families were moved out of
London altogether, with places as far apart as Manchester, Hastings,
Pembrokeshire, Dover and Newcastle receiving families. Changes to the
benefits cap in 2016 will affect more families across the country, with
around 116,000 families affected nationwide, including, for example,
around 5,000 families in the north-east and around 12,000 families in
the north-west.[28]

Many regeneration schemes, such as those proposed by Cameron
in his sink estates speech, have seen public housing demolished or
refurbished and reallocated or sold as private properties. Up and down
the country over recent years, government regeneration schemes have
seen families relocated, sometimes with the promise of a return 'home'
at an unspecified later date. Communities have been promised a 'new
deal' in some areas, whilst others have been the alleged beneficiaries of
the rather blunter Housing Market Renewal Initiative. Invariably, and
whatever marketing gloss is applied to the scheme, many low-income
families are forced out of their homes and many never make it back, with
far fewer social housing properties available following 'regeneration'
than there were before.

Such programmes of 'regeneration' often equate to attempts to
create purified spaces on a much larger scale than the poor doors that
keep affordable housing tenants out of the executive entrance lobbies
frequented by private owners and renters. The state is withdrawing

or reducing its material and physical presence in certain areas where it believes 'the market' is better placed to bring about growth and 'renewal'. Public support from, and encounters with, the state in such areas become less frequent. Elements of financial support are removed or capped. Public buildings are closed or their opening hours and access arrangements are reduced. Neighbourhood-based staff are relocated to other buildings or merged in 'centralised' teams.

In *The Weight of the World*, Pierre Bourdieu argues that American ghettos are 'abandoned sites that are fundamentally defined by an absence' of state institutions and the services and resources that they bring with them.[29] More recently, Loic Wacquant has argued, again about ghettos in America, that there has been a 'policy of malign neglect by the state on the housing, welfare and taxation front', and that this neglect 'does not stop at welfare policy but extends to the gamut of services aimed at disadvantaged populations'.[30] This turnaround of neighbourhood-based services has occurred at the same time that the state has been simultaneously increasing its reach into the private homes and spaces of disadvantaged families. In the past, when home-based interventions were on the increase, it was often part of a wider expansion of welfare activities.

The social-work academic Harry Ferguson has highlighted how, in the early years of the twentieth century, the home visit became a fundamental part of the burgeoning practice of attempting to protect children from abuse and neglect.[31] He quotes a 1904 practitioner manual of the National Society for the Prevention of Cruelty to Children, which states that getting access to the house 'will depend on determination and tact' and that 'no difficulty will be too great where these exist'.[32] Similarly, and at around the same time, the practice of making health visits was also emerging, with arrangements in Manchester and Salford in the 1860s summed up as 'visits to working-class homes by Christian women who would give advice on domestic arrangements and "tender and sympathetic remonstrance" to the intemperate'.[33] A key aspect of early health visits was ensuring that houses were kept clean and, where health visitors lived in the same district as the women they visited, it was expected that their homes would serve as 'an object lesson in cleanliness, tidiness, etc., to the neighbours'.[34] In the 1940s and 1950s, the proposed solution to an alleged group of 'problem families' was a system of family support that helped with domestic routines and was characterised as offering 'friendship with a purpose' to the mothers in those families.[35]

Today, however, the expansion of programmes and policies which prioritise interventions that take place in family settings is concurrent with the withdrawal of much of the state's other welfare activities. In recent years, a number of new programmes of work have been based around home visiting. The Family Nurse Partnership approach aims to work with young mothers and mothers-to-be to support them and their babies and is based around frequent intensive and structured home visits.[36] The Troubled Families Programme is based on a model of 'family intervention' that requires a 'dedicated' key worker to be persistent, assertive and challenging in their dealings with 'troubled families', with a lot of the political focus on work that takes place inside the family home and the quality of the relationship built up between worker and family members.[37] At the launch of the programme, David Cameron argued that it would help to deliver better coordination of public services and emphasise support with practical, domestic chores:

> When the front door opens and the worker goes in, they will see the family as a whole and get a plan of action together, agreed with the family. This will often be basic, practical things – like getting the kids to school on time, properly fed – that are the building blocks of an orderly home and a responsible life.[38]

Louise Casey, the former director general of the Troubled Families Unit of the Department for Communities and Local Government, has also argued that it is the ability to work with, and assertively challenge, if not threaten families in the intimate space of the front room that is key to the 'family intervention' approach:

> What we know works is this thing called family intervention and what it does is basically get into the actual family, in their front room and if actually the kids aren't in school it gets in there and says to the parents I'm gonna show you and explain to you exactly how to get your kids up and out every single day and then I'm gonna make you do it. And if you don't do it, there are gonna be consequences.[39]

The rhetorical focus on the state needing to get in through the front door and into the front room to help implement domestic routines helps to augment the discourse that circulates around poor or 'troubled' families in the UK at the current time. Families are alleged to 'sit at home' all day on the 'sofa of despair'. The identification of private spaces of the family home as being problematic, albeit in different ways, serves to legitimate the intervention of the state, both symbolically and literally, in these spaces. At the same time, this political gaze on the personal spaces of disadvantaged families conveniently deflects attention away from the retreat of the state in other areas of public service provision. Children's centres are not needed if families can be worked with in their homes.

The political and physical extension of state involvement in the lives of 'troubled families' at the same time that other, universal welfare programmes are being rolled back is an example of what Loic Wacquant has called the 'remasculinisation' of the state.[40] He argues that a 'thick' version of neoliberalism that accounts for the state's increasingly intrusive interventions into the lives of poor and marginalised populations (via a shift from welfare policies to workfare programmes) is preferable to the dominant 'thin' perspective of neoliberalism, which sees neoliberalism primarily as a free-market ideology that advocates 'small government'. He argues that:

> while it [the neoliberal state] embraces laissez-faire at the top, releasing restraints on capital and expanding the life chances of the holders of economic and cultural capital, it is anything but laissez-faire at the bottom. Indeed, when it comes to handling the social turbulence generated by deregulation and to impressing the discipline of precarious labour, the new Leviathan reveals itself to be fiercely interventionist, bossy, and pricey. The soft touch of libertarian proclivities favouring the upper class gives way to the hard edge of authoritarian oversight, as it endeavours to direct, nay dictate, the behaviour of the lower class.[41]

Whilst Wacquant focuses primarily on workfare schemes to regulate the job-seeking activity of marginalised groups in the United States, his analysis also appears particularly relevant to the Troubled Families Programme (TFP) and other family- and poverty-related programmes in the UK. The concept of the 'remasculinisation' of the state is also particularly appropriate given the often hands-on practical nature of the work associated with the TFP. Family workers, according to the official rhetoric, are expected to be able to help and then ensure mothers get children ready for school, cook meals for the family, clean the house, improve and maintain personal hygiene standards and establish bedtime routines for children where appropriate. Domestic routines and chores carried out within the house still tend to be associated with mothers more than with fathers. A rhetorical preoccupation with lone mothers and fathers who are absent at best cements the image of the homes of 'troubled families' as heavily gendered spaces. The idea that effective family workers 'grip' the family and all their problems similarly brings to mind a physical, muscular approach to 'tackling' the families' problems, which are thus located as the outcome of maternal weaknesses, failings or incompetence. By infantilising the parents in 'troubled families', making it appear that they are completely incapable of bringing up children without the support of the state, this narrative serves to augment the political interest in 'parenting' and 'early intervention' as the best ways of improving children's lives. They also draw attention specifically to the role of mothers.

The emphasis on practical, hands-on support that takes place in the family home also helps to shift attention away from other bureaucratic practices associated with the TFP, some of which rely on activity of a much more impersonal nature, taking place far away from the front room of 'troubled families' and the 'street level' more usually associated with public services. The portrayal of the TFP as a policy which recognises the importance of face-to-face human interactions belies the importance of cold, hard data to the programme.

TOWARDS A 'VIRTUAL BUREAUCRACY'?

The state's desire to collect information on 'troublesome' or 'problematic' populations is, of course, nothing new.[42] In more recent times, in the early 2000s, the New Labour government in the UK developed and pursued 'a radical programme to redesign the apparatus of government through the use of information and communication technologies (ICTs)'.[43] Their 'e-galitarianism' agenda required greater sharing of data between agencies and was linked to the perceived need to reduce public expenditure whilst providing a better 'targeted' service for those in most need.[44] In a strong critique of the call for 'joined-up thinking' around children 'at risk' or 'in need', the critical social work academic Paul Garrett argued, 'the databases now provided for the Children Act 2004 appear to be an invitation for "virtual" cabals of professionals to cluster and reach decisions in secret'.[45] Displaying commendable foresight, Garrett went on to argue, 'Perhaps there should also be concern about the "function creep" potential of the databases in a social context where ideas about "problem families" are returning to popular, political and professional debates'.[46]

Personal data on 'troubled families' must be checked to ensure they are sufficiently 'troubled' to meet the criteria for inclusion on the TFP, and those data are checked again at the point where they are believed to have been 'turned around' to ensure that they have met the targets for a 'payment by results' claim. In the first phase of the TFP, local authorities were required to collect 55 pieces of information about all members of a household across domains such as family details, education, training and employment, housing and child protection, crime and anti-social behaviour and health. This information was required for the official evaluation of the programme. There were 18 different indicators in the health section alone, despite health issues forming no part of the national criteria for being identified as a 'troubled family' in Phase 1. The linking of one or more individual's behaviour with a presumed wider household malaise meant that siblings, parents or partners living in the same household had their details collected, stored and shared by the state even if they had not engaged in any 'troublesome' behaviour.

The expanded second phase of the TFP, which has seen an additional 400,000 families classified as 'troubled', has introduced new criteria and more data collection requirements and data-sharing issues. The Department for Communities and Local Government has published a guidance document for local authorities, in which it outlines ways in which they can safely and legally share families' data with other government departments and partner agencies, along with a separate 'interim guidance' document for health professionals to assist them in 'sharing health information about patients and service users with troubled families'.[47]

Individuals are asked to contact their local authority if they want to know if their data are being used as part of the project but, given that a large number of local authorities do not tell the families they are working with that they are classed as 'troubled families' and most authorities call their local programmes by different names, many families will not know that they are part of the TFP in the first place. In a highly ironic twist, local authorities have been advised to display posters in 'public places', which presumably includes spaces such as children's centres, community centres and libraries, as well as on council websites, in order to inform families that their data may be used for the evaluation.

There are other examples of increasing amounts of data on poor and marginalised groups being captured and stored by the state. The Universal Jobmatch IT system, provided by the private sector company Monster, which encourages, if not mandates, jobseekers to carry out all of their job search activity online, provides the state with all of the information it needs in deciding whether to sanction an individual (withdraw their entitlement to benefits for a period of time) for not meeting their requirements.[48] The Sodexo probation example, mentioned earlier, also highlights just how private sector firms are becoming more involved with public services, not just at 'street level' but also in the 'back room'.

The need to collect, share, store and analyse large amounts of highly sensitive data has led to a number of private sector, sometimes multi-national, software companies and management consultancies circling around local authorities, offering software packages and database designs that can 'help'. One company claims: 'Ultimately the technology will allow authority staff to create a holistic view of a family', with it being 'vital that technology continues to provide the critical backbone support teams need to help them build a much brighter future for some of the most vulnerable families in society'.[49] Data-matching exercises to identify potential 'troubled families' has been likened to a form of 'algorithmic pre-emption' by the social-computing academic Dan McQuillan, who has highlighted the way that new developments in database structures and data-mining techniques are leading to new forms of 'computational government'.[50]

One English local authority has contracted with a Silicon Valley firm called Palantir,[51] best known for its work with the American military and intelligence services such as the National Security Agency, the CIA and the FBI to develop an 'intelligence hub' for the city. The local authority claims, in somewhat Orwellian language, that this 'strategic partnership' will 'help us better understand our customers and communities, their needs and patterns of behaviour, and how they go about their business'.[52]

Palantir's headquarters are in Palo Alto, California, and they have offices in nine different countries. They have fanned rumours that have suggested that their software was used in the targeting of Osama Bin Laden when he was killed.[53] They have been described as 'a CIA-funded data-mining juggernaut'.[54] On their website, the first image that visitors are greeted with is of armed combat troops marching through a barren environment. Their primary products are called Gotham and Metropolis, and in one article in *Forbes* magazine, influential American government and military figures such as Condoleeza Rice and Dan Petraeus provided glowing praise for Palantir and their work in fighting terrorists and combating crime.[55] In a remarkable twist, the 'weapons' that were developed to target 'exotic' Others are now being deployed to identify domestic and more 'familiar' Others.

All of this seems a very long way from the intimate domestic encounter between 'family worker' and 'troubled family' that is allegedly at the heart of the TFP. Nor does it neatly match Louise Casey's suggestion that the missing ingredient in the state's engagement with 'troubled families' is 'love'.[56] The involvement of national and international private sector companies in the storage and analysis of data further adds to the view that the 'front rooms' of 'troubled families' are not the only, or perhaps even the best, spaces to study the implementation of the TFP. The spaces where decisions about 'who gets what' is shifting from the street to the 'cloud', and the dilemmas faced by individuals in public services are increasingly being resolved by algorithms that precious few citizens, or street-level bureaucrats for that matter, currently understand.

RE-CRAFTING AND RESHAPING THE STATE

This chapter has explored the ways in which the spaces of the state are shifting. At the same time that the ideological re-crafting of the state is witnessing the withdrawal of supportive welfarist state services from dis-advantaged neighbourhoods on both sides of the Atlantic, increasingly intrusive policies aimed at managing and controlling marginalised populations are being rolled out. Welfare reforms in the UK in recent years have 'hit the poorest places hardest' and have targeted the most disadvantaged families as well. The withdrawal of the state from neigh-bourhoods and other public spaces, as local authorities attempt to manage their budgets in the face of unprecedented cuts, has come as the state simultaneously extends its reach into the private physical and virtual spaces of the most 'troubled' and disadvantaged families. The spatial shifts highlighted in this chapter reflect 'the correlative revamping of the perimeter missions, and capacities of public authority on the economic, social welfare and penal fronts'.[57]

Encounters between citizen and state are, rhetorically at least, increasingly likely to take place in the highly gendered domestic spaces of marginalised families which helps to focus political and public attention on the role of working-class women and mothers in particular in maintaining social order, or in 'the cloud', where algorithms will help to target certain groups for 'early intervention'. The tech-savvy, muscular, persistent, assertive and challenging approach to allegedly troublesome families in England highlights the way in which the neoliberal state is being 'remasculinised'. The withdrawal of the state from public spaces and its re-emergence in private spaces and password-protected virtual spaces should concern us, especially at a time when the private lives of marginalised groups are increasingly coming under media, political and public scrutiny.

9
Studying Up

Of all the classes, the wealthy are the most noticed and least studied.

J. K. Galbraith, 1977.[1]

In the 1960s and 1970s, the Chicago community organiser Saul Alinsky popularised a story that has sometimes been referred to as 'the parable of the river'. There are a few variations, but it goes something like this: There are a group of campers on a river bank, enjoying the scenery and relaxing when one of them notices a baby in the water, floating downstream. A camper jumps in, rescues the baby and brings the child to the shore, where the rest of the campers help to make sure it is okay. A short while later, another camper notices two babies in the water. Again, a camper jumps in, the babies are rescued and brought to the shore, where they are looked after. Shortly afterwards, three babies are spotted, and so it continues. The campers develop into an effective life-saving team, rescuing lots of babies and caring for them once they are out of the water. More people come to help when they see what is happening although, unfortunately, the numbers of babies in the water grows to the stage where not all of them can be saved.

At this point, one of the campers leaves the group and starts walking upstream along the river bank. Her friends ask where she is going, pointing out that they need her more than ever. She stops, looks at her friends and says. 'We need to find out who's throwing all these babies in.'[2]

This book has highlighted that it is the downstream areas that attract much of the attention when discussions about what causes poverty and how to solve it take place, which was precisely the point Alinksy was making. Very rarely does anyone – a politician, a journalist, or a researcher – venture upstream to find out why so many people are living in poverty. The American sociologist Gary T. Marx remarked, appropriately, that, '[l]ike a river, researchers follow the path of least resistance' and rarely go where they were not welcome or where they are not at least tolerated.[3] This chapter argues that as well as the 'rescue efforts' taking place downstream, we are in urgent need of far more upstream exploration and action.

Following a brief summary of the spaces discussed in the previous chapters and the arguments advanced in this book, attention turns to some preparatory groundwork that has been, and is currently being, carried out in efforts to excavate different upstream spaces. The argument is made that we must explicitly link the behaviour of rich and powerful groups in society with the conditions experienced by marginalised and less powerful groups. This can only be done by interrogating the spaces where they live and where they make decisions that affect the structure and stratification of society.

In the previous chapters we have examined a variety of imagined geographies and spaces that are traditionally associated or symbolically linked with discourses about poverty. In Chapter 2, the use of exotic and other worldly images was explored, drawing on various historical and contemporary attempts to depict the poor as a source of fascination and as an exotic, primitive or alien species. People living in poverty in the UK have been compared to African pygmies, savages and animals, and the places where they reside have been represented as akin to 'fetid swamps', 'twilight worlds' and a 'world that is unrecognisable'.

Chapter 3 discussed the ways in which spaces in different cities were depicted, with a contrast made between cities struggling economically with the effects of deindustrialisation, and those that were portrayed as vibrant centres of culture and opportunity. Residents of towns and cities like Detroit and Middlesbrough are portrayed as being 'backward', lacking in entrepreneurial skills and aspiration, devoid of the cultural capital of 'clever' outsiders. Attempts by cities such as Newcastle, Glasgow and London to remake their image often rely on the physical and social exclusion of marginalised groups from city-centre locations as the state and private capital combine to create, sustain and promote city centres as vibrant 'purified spaces'.

Attempts to represent disadvantaged neighbourhoods and 'the street' or street corners by different groups were discussed in the fourth and fifth chapters. The use of poor urban areas by politicians, as 'political settings' for important speeches, policy announcements or personal distinction or reinvention, was discussed. Dealing in territorial stigmatisation, these politicians often attempt implicitly to highlight the neighbourhood effects thesis and minimise the effect that Westminster policies have on the lives of disadvantaged populations. Two different forms of street sociology and criminology were discussed in Chapter 5, which highlighted the differences between researchers who focused on 'the street' and trained their eyes primarily on the daily comings and goings of residents or gang members, and those who used street settings, and adopted a 'street-level lens' to better understand wider structural and societal changes. A further, complementary distinction was made between an ethnographic approach that offers a 'thick description' of daily life in marginalised communities and one that aims for a 'thick construction' of the wider conditions that structure and impinge on those residents that live in disadvantaged areas.

The 'heroic simplification' of the household in poverty measurement research and anti-poverty policies was explored in Chapter 6. The gender neutral space of 'the household' masks the disproportionate poverty burden and risk borne by women, and contains problematic assumptions about intra-household income distribution and the extent to which women have access to, or control over, income that comes into the house in different ways. Whilst measurements of poverty, and income-related efforts to tackle it often stop at the front door of low-income households, judgements about poor families permeate every room in the house. Chapter 7 examined some of the imagined spaces behind closed doors in poor families' homes, highlighting the stigmatising representations and fantasies of 'sofas of despair', meals of 'cheese and chips in Styrofoam containers', sitting rooms full of 'piles of Pringles and crack' and 'massive fucking TVs' that dominate discourses about the domestic spaces of families living in poverty. The circulation of these discourses and the increasing pathologisation of poverty helps to legitimise the state intervention in the family home discussed in Chapter 8, which is aimed at bringing about behaviour change and uses a 'persistent, assertive and challenging' approach in a concerted government effort to motivate people out of poverty. This increased presence in the domestic and personal sphere of poor families' lives, accompanied by an increase in the amount of data being collected on marginalised groups, comes at the same time that the state is retreating from previous traditional public spaces and buildings.

A key theme in these discussions has been the focus on and representation of local and everyday spaces associated with people living in poverty. Politicians, journalists, social reformers and researchers have all left their enclaves and visited or 'toured' places of poverty in order to get a better handle on what to do about it. In doing so, cities in which large numbers of low-income households can be found are represented as places on their last legs, devoid of culture and civilisation; the neighbourhoods in which some poor people live are represented as 'dreadful enclosures', 'sink estates' or 'twilight worlds'; and the kitchens of disadvantaged families are represented as places where, for instance, dangerous-looking dogs are kept. More intangible structural disadvantages such as poverty, inequality and material deprivation are cleverly repackaged and represented, using material spaces, as behavioural problems caused by 'bad' attitudes and dispositions that seep into people from their surroundings, and are exacerbated by the 'wrong' 'lifestyle choices' made within the family home.

That these local spaces are the ones that need to be visited, researched and written about is taken for granted and accepted largely without question. Ever since William Booth marked out different poverty-stricken neighbourhoods in London in the 1880s in his colour-coded maps, the need to 'go and see things close up' and 'first hand' has rarely been challenged. Hand-drawn boundaries on a map are, however, no longer required. Symbolic and material markers highlight the transition from an affluent and middle-class area that might 'feel' relatively safe to one that is perceived and presented as poorer, possibly more dangerous and definitely more deviant. Tower block: tick. Young people on street corners: tick. Untidy gardens: tick. These alleged signifiers of poverty and deviance are embedded in the publics minds and, according to Bourdieu, operate as a screen whose 'great strength lies in how obvious it seems because it is so close to the discourse of common sense'.[4] Of course, social housing estates will often contain more people on low incomes than private housing estates or gated communities. Of course, young people hanging around on street corners may be there because they do not have the resources to access other, usually private sector, leisure spaces. But that does not mean that the people frequenting these spaces, or indeed the spaces themselves, represent a threat to society or are any more a source of deviancy than other, less symbolically potent spaces. Writing about the role of academics in uncovering the real social and political determinants of people's lives, Bourdieu argued that it was 'necessary to break through the screen of often absurd, sometime odious projections, that mask the malaise or suffering as much as they express it'.[5]

If these damaging and pernicious imagined spaces of poverty and deviance are to be challenged, we need to train our eyes on new spaces that have escaped the spotlight for too long and highlight the role that other spaces play in creating poverty. Just as Bourdieu warned against researchers simply ratifying the social problems gifted to them by powerful institutions and argued for research that 'twists the stick in the other direction',[6] other sociologists, anthropologists, geographers and activists have made the case for 'studying up' and subjecting new spaces and different populations to a critical gaze. A focus on more affluent spaces, such as the trading floors of stock exchanges, the boardrooms of multinational companies and the 'corridors of power' in Westminster, would help to highlight how locales truly can affect the conditions under which people live their lives.

<h2 style="text-align:center">'REVERSING THE MACHINERY'</h2>

In 1968, an American sociology student called Martin Nicolaus gave an extraordinary address at an American Sociological Association convention, incensed at the invitation of William Cohen, the secretary of health education and welfare, to the event. During his address, which came to be known as the 'fat-cat sociology speech', Nicolaus stated:

> The department of which the man [Cohen] is head is more accurately described as the agency which watches over the inequitable distribution of preventable disease, over the funding of domestic propaganda and indoctrination, and over the preservation of a cheap and docile reserve labour force to keep everybody else's wages down. He is the Secretary of disease, propaganda, and scabbing.[7]

Cohen and his government department were not the only targets of Nicolaus's ire. He raged against 'the honoured sociologist, the big-status sociologist, the jet-set sociologist' whose 'eyes ... have been turned downward, and their palms upward'. He went on, in a passage that was doubtless aimed at 'street sociologists' like some of those of the Chicago School:

> The more adventurous sociologists don the disguise of the people and go out and mix with the peasants in the 'field', returning with books and articles that break the protective secrecy in which a subjugated population wraps itself, and make it more accessible to manipulation and control.

His speech, however, was not solely a critique of the state of affairs of American sociology in the 1960s. He also offered a perspective on an alternative approach and how to address the issues he spoke of, posing a question about the potential to alter the one-way flow of knowledge 'from the people ... to the rulers':

> What if that machinery were reversed? What if the habits, problems, secrets, and unconscious motivations of the wealthy and powerful were daily scrutinized by a thousand systematic researchers, were hourly pried into, analysed and cross-referenced; were tabulated and published in a hundred inexpensive mass-circulation journals and written so that even the fifteen-year-old high-school drop-out could understand them and predict the actions of his landlord to manipulate and control him?

A few years later, in 1972, the American anthropologist Laura Nader made similar influential remarks about the need to 'study up', highlighting that there was an abundance of academic literature on poor populations but a dearth of information that had been gained by studies of the rich. She asked what if anthropologists 'were to study the colonisers rather than the colonised, the culture of power rather than the culture of the powerless, the culture of affluence rather that the culture of poverty?'[8] Nader argued that 'studying up' would lead researchers to ask 'commonsense' questions in reverse, such as, instead of asking why people are poor, asking why people are affluent. Instead of enquiries into scarcity and material deprivation, Nader suggested looking at the 'hoarding patterns' of the American middle classes. Instead of describing the conditions of slum neighbourhoods, researchers should be examining the behaviour of landlords, building officials and enforcement officers who allowed such neighbourhoods to proliferate. Or they should be asking how business crime affects street crime. Adopting this perspective would force researchers and other interested parties, such as politicians and policymakers, to question the narrow-minded, and spatially-bounded, view that the conditions in which poor people live and the behaviour they exhibit are largely the products of a culture of poverty or similar.

Recently, perhaps as a result of increasing inequality, or perhaps because a number of powerful individuals and institutions have been shown to have their own shortcomings, people have been 'studying up' a little more, and there has been a growing interest in how what the Occupy movement dubbed the '1%' live, and how it affects the rest of us. Investigative journalists have uncovered MPs' fraudulent and duplicitous expenses claims, including the practice of 'flipping' their homes in order to claim the maximum amount possible for their mortgages.[9] Following the MPs expenses scandal in 2009, it emerged that politicians had attempted to charge the public purse for items as diverse as a floating duck island costing over £1,500, and a car journey of less than four hundred metres, equating to 8p.[10] Iain Duncan Smith, in charge of reducing welfare spending in the coalition government, attempted to claim £39 for a breakfast during the time he was in opposition.[11] A few years later, the unhealthy relationship between some politicians, members of the press and police officers was also uncovered via the phone hacking scandal and the revelations that followed.[12] The regulatory system and political oversight of our financial institutions were shown to be flawed by the financial crisis that took place in 2007/8, and which our economy is still to recover from.[13] In addition to the reckless institutionalised gambling that led to the crash, we have since heard about other misdemeanours, including efforts by bankers in certain banks to rig the Libor rate, which has implications for the lending rates of banks for items such as student loans, mortgages and other financial products.[14]

The scandal of off-shore banking has also been uncovered recently, with the leaking and publishing of the so-called Panama Papers, highlighting the lengths that many individuals and corporations go to in order to avoid paying various forms of tax on their assets and savings.[15] It was revealed that David Cameron received a £200,000 gift from his mother via an offshore fund that meant he did not have to pay inheritance tax.[16] Essentially, it was revealed that the man responsible for the health and well-being of the country, whose estimated wealth is around £10 million,[17] and who once rose from a gold chair to deliver a speech from a gold lectern about the need for permanent austerity,[18] had deliberately avoided paying £80,000 in tax.

The tax affairs of multinational corporations have also been subjected to recent scrutiny. Google, whose motto is 'do no evil', struggled to articulate how that motto fitted with their attempts to avoid paying tax in the UK, and in light of the fact that they agreed to pay £130 million in back taxes on a revenue stream of around £4.9 billion in 2012.[19] The current president of the United States, Donald Trump, remarked that the fact his company had not paid any federal tax for over 20 years proved that he was 'smart'.[20] He remains one of only two presidential candidates of the last 40 years not to publish his tax affairs whilst running for office.

Danny Dorling has made the point that economists have been measuring the incomes of the richest 1 per cent for many years, but it is only recently that journalists, activists and campaigners have become similarly interested.[21] Dorling has also highlighted that, for many members of the 1 per cent, use of state services in education and health, for example, is 'unusual' and that they are likely to inhabit different spaces, in many ways, to members of the other 99 per cent. A similar point has been made regarding members of London's 'super rich', people whose wealth is so great that shops will open out of hours to allow them to purchase items without having to be around other people. The resources and services they have access to in their home, such as private chefs, cinemas and gyms, ensure that such people have little need to share *any* public spaces with Others. Recent research has also highlighted that the neighbourhoods where the super rich live are becoming 'gilded ghettos' – gated communities where private security guards operate – and where the state, as Bourdieu and Wacquant note of American ghettos, is fundamentally absent.[22] If there really is a group of people cut off from the rest of society, unable or unwilling to integrate into the 'mainstream', and whose behaviour represents a potential threat to social solidarity, we may have been looking for them in the wrong places.

These stories and revelations stand out as exceptions to the majority of material that we read about in newspapers, books or academic journals, and that we see or hear about on television and radio. But what if these standout stories and pieces of research became the norm? What if, as Martin Nicolaus urged, the machinery was reversed? What if the researchers who spent so much time looking at the street focused their attention on 'the boulevards' and 'the avenue' instead? What if, for example, instead of examining and criticising the eating habits of people forced to live on an income that the government acknowledges places them in poverty, we examined the eating and drinking habits of the MPs who consumed around £7 million – or £11,000 per MP – in food and drink in Parliament alone in 2013, despite ushering in a period of austerity for other groups that were largely dependent on the state for their income?

As well as documenting the poor and overcrowded housing conditions that many people on low incomes experience, researchers and reporters should be documenting the housing conditions and interests of those who voted to place a cap on benefits that a single household can receive, and who also voted against introducing regulations that would ensure private rented accommodation was fit for human habitation.[23] In addition to researching how people living in poverty struggle to manage their money and cover their expenditures, we should also study how those politicians who decide that it is perfectly acceptable, in the twenty-first century, to force people to live on incomes that are often insufficient to allow them to meet their basic needs, spend their own incomes, and how they behave at home 'behind closed doors'.

Imagine if those individuals and corporations that are capable of avoiding or evading the tax that they owe, or squirreling their money away 'offshore', were subject to the same scrutiny as those accused of 'fiddling the dole'. In 2016, Her Majesty's Revenue and Customs estimated that the 'tax gap', the difference between the amount of tax that should be paid and that which is actually collected, was around £36 billion.[24] This is a conservative estimate, and the tax specialist and Professor at City University, London, Richard Murphy has argued that the tax gap is actually closer to £120 billion.[25] A report published in October 2016 by the National Audit Office showed that despite an increase in the number of 'high-net worth individuals' in the UK (someone with wealth of more than £20 million) since 2009, the amount of tax paid by the super rich had actually fallen by £900 million to £3.5 billion.[26] The actual cost of ending poverty in the UK is not known, but in 2006, when child poverty figures were slightly higher than they are at the current time, research published by the Joseph Rowntree Foundation estimated that it would cost around £28 billion to end child poverty.[27] This was an estimate of perhaps the most expensive way of ending poverty, by simply transferring sufficient income to those living in poverty to ensure that they no longer did so. Other ways, such as creating more jobs, and improving the pay, security and conditions of existing jobs, would potentially lead to the cost, to the government, of ending poverty being substantially lower.

The idea of the government 'handing out' money to people on low incomes to eradicate poverty may not be a palatable choice to many people, worried about increasing 'welfare dependency', but it is undeniable that it is an option.[28] The government have it within their gift to end poverty immediately if they so wished. People can argue against the wisdom or otherwise of doing so, but it cannot be argued that it is not within their power, and it would be a strange argument that suggested consequences of ending poverty would be greater than the consequences of allowing it to endure.

Politicians do not need to travel to the Aylesbury Estate or Easterhouse to learn about what to do about poverty. They can do it from Westminster. There is significant research from comparative and international studies of poverty rates that demonstrate, beyond doubt, that it is possible to design, develop and implement a social system where far fewer people, proportionately speaking, suffer from the effects of poverty. European countries as diverse as Austria, Denmark, France and Slovakia all have significantly lower poverty rates than the UK, despite all having smaller economies.[29] If Westminster politicians were at all interested in tackling inequality, they could easily attempt to examine the policies pursued by countries such as Japan, Korea and Sweden, which all have far lower levels of economic inequality than the UK.[30] If researchers need to get used to 'studying up', politicians and policymakers would do well to stop 'looking down' and start 'looking out', preferably to countries in Scandinavia, mainland Europe and parts of the Far East.

THE OVERCLASS

A research focus on powerful groups and the spaces they operate in can help us to understand why poverty continues to exist. It is not, and never has been, because of the alleged behaviours of 'an underclass' or whatever label has been attached to a contemporary version of the 'undeserving poor', living in slums, 'delinquent areas' or 'problem neighbourhoods'. Poverty has been allowed to flourish in one of the richest countries in the world not because of an alleged lack of culinary skills and moral fibre amongst working-class women, but because a relatively small number of powerful people, usually men, have chosen to do very little, if anything, about it. In fact, in recent years, given that it is widely known and accepted that child poverty in the UK is likely to rise in the lead up to 2020, primarily as a result of the tax and benefit changes introduced by the coalition government,[31] it is fairly safe to assert that politicians have actively chosen to oversee an increase in poverty. That has been their choice.

In the early 1990s, Peter Townsend made the point that the 'overclass' – the powerful vested interests that profit from poverty – deserved as much attention as any putative 'underclass'. He argued powerfully, in words which continue to be relevant today, for linking security and prosperity with poverty, but also highlighted how other sections of society secured or enhanced their position at the expense of the poorest sections:

> We must not make the mistake of supposing that the growth of poverty has been accidental, unintended and merely a by-product of economic or technological change. It is the logical, indeed inevitable, result of strategies of self-aggrandisement and cost or damage limitation followed by corporate enterprises and wealth-holders, but also, to a lesser extent, by the professions and bureaucratic organisations which largely serve them. There is a danger in only blaming a distant state capitalism for the growth of poverty. Responsibility also resides in professions, unions and other administrative organisations for many actions which have furthered their own material prosperity and status at the indirect and sometimes direct expense of impoverished minorities. The gulf between relatively secure and certainly prosperous professionals and administrative staff and their poorest clients has widened sharply in the last few years. Dependency and deprivation have been created on a big scale in recent years.[32]

Despite the increased interest in researching and reporting the lives of the powerful, there has been little connection between these pieces of work and more traditional poverty-related research. In 2013, following a two-day workshop, and as part of efforts to develop a comprehensive anti-poverty strategy for the UK, the Joseph Rowntree Foundation, one of the biggest funders of poverty research in the UK, published a list of 100 questions identifying research priorities for poverty prevention and reduction. Of these, only one out of the hundred related to powerful, vested interests: 'Who benefits from poverty, and how?'[33] Whilst others focused on examining the role of issues such as attitudes towards poverty, education and employment, there was no suggestion that it would be entirely appropriate to attempt to systematically gather information with the aim of understanding the role of powerful decision-makers who enable poverty to continue. The lives of people living in poverty need to be linked to the lives of those enjoying positions of power.

Doing this will not necessarily, or magically, make poverty disappear, certainly not overnight. There will be, and always has been, resistance amongst powerful groups to attempts at highlighting the ways in which their power and prosperity depend on others enduring poverty and relative powerlessness. Late in life, Pierre Bourdieu set out the suffering experienced by marginalised groups in France and America, arguing that 'producing awareness of these mechanisms that makes life painful, even unliveable, does not neutralize them'.[34] Nor, however, did he argue that the observation was 'cause for despair', arguing that 'what the social world has done, it can, armed with this knowledge, undo ... [I]n any event, what is certain is that nothing is less innocent than non-interference'.[35]

If, as a society, we still believe it is possible and worthwhile to eradicate poverty, we can do so. In terms of the economics of the situation, it is relatively easy to achieve. Politicians and policymakers in other countries as we have seen have managed to achieve and maintain lower levels of poverty and inequality than we have. But we cannot understand the reasons *why* people remain in poverty by focusing on the spaces they inhabit, reside in and frequent. We must turn our attention to less-researched and under-reported spaces. Lucy Parsons, the radical American socialist and community organiser, argued that, 'every dirty, lousy tramp [should] arm himself with a revolver or knife and lay in wait on the steps of the palaces of the rich' and take direct and violent action as it was necessary to 'devastate the avenues where the wealthy live'.[36] Not everyone will agree with such violence, but many would agree that arming reporters and researchers with pens, notebooks and tape recorders in an attempt to interrogate the avenues where the wealthy live, prying into their daily routines and scrutinising their 'lifestyle choices', as well as their 'policy choices', would be a good start.

Notes

CHAPTER 1

1. P. Bourdieu, 'Physical Space, Social Space and Habitus', *Rapport* 10 (1996): 7–22, quote from p. 11.
2. N. Thrift, 'Space: The Fundamental Stuff of Human Geography', in N. Clifford, S. Holloway, S.P. Rice and G. Valentine (eds), *Key Concepts in Geography*, 2nd edn (London: Sage, 2009), pp. 95–107, quote from p. 95.
3. D. Massey, *For Space* (London: Sage, 2005), p. 1.
4. P. Golding and S. Middleton, *Images of Welfare: Press and Public Attitudes to Poverty* (Oxford: Martin Robertson, 1982), p. 186.
5. R. Lister, *Poverty* (Cambridge: Polity Press, 2004), p. 101.
6. Baroness Lister is perhaps better known as Ruth Lister, Professor of Social Policy at Loughborough University, and who was previously director of the Child Poverty Action Group. The use of a capital 'O' in Othering in this book follows Lister's practice, which highlights the symbolic weight of the concept.
7. C. Petonnet, *Those People: The Subculture of a Housing Project* (Westport, CT: Greenwood Press, 1973), p. xxi.
8. D. Cameron, 'Troubled Families Speech', 15 December 2011 (available at: https://www.gov.uk/government/speeches/troubled-families-speech, accessed 13 March 2017).
9. For a fuller critique of the misrepresentation of this research and the conflation of 'poor families' with 'poorly behaved families', see R. Levitas, 'There May Be "Trouble" Ahead: What We Know about Those 120,000 "Troubled" Families', Policy Response Series No. 3, Poverty and Social Exclusion in the UK, 2012 (available at: http://www.poverty.ac.uk/system/files/WP%20Policy%20Response%20No.3-%20%20%27Trouble%27%20 ahead%20(Levitas%20Final%2021April2012).pdf, accessed 13 March 2017).
10. J. Welshman, *Underclass: A History of the Excluded Since 1880*, 2nd edn (London: Bloomsbury, 2013).
11. H. Glennerster, J. Hills, D. Piachaud and J. Webb, 'One Hundred Years Of Poverty and Policy' (York: Joseph Rowntree Foundation, 2004).
12. There is an emerging literature on 'over-researched' communities, and Danny Dorling has pointed out that many geography undergraduate courses take students, complete with clipboards, on field trips to study disadvantaged neighbourhoods. In an examination of such neighbourhoods, Sarah Neal et al. claimed that 'young people who lived in a deprived residential area behind Kings Cross Station in London, were so used to the presence of researchers that they would confidently ask new researchers about their project's methods and ethical protocols' – S. Neal, G. Mohan, A. Cochrane and K. Bennett,

"'You Can't Move in Hackney without Bumping into an Anthropologist":
Why Certain Places Attract Research Attention', *Qualitative Research* 16/5
(2016): 491–507, quote from p. 492.

13. Macintyre is an investigative journalist who specialised in the early 2000s in
'going undercover' in dangerous situations. His attempt to highlight street
crime in London for a BBC series in 2002 was roundly criticised for the
lengths to which Macintyre went in order to ensure the expensive laptop he
was carrying around with him actually got stolen.

14. P. Bourdieu et al., *The Weight of the World: Social Suffering in Contemporary
Society* (Cambridge: Polity Press, 1999), p. 123.

15. D. Sibley, *Geographies of Exclusion: Society and Difference in the West* (London:
Routledge, 1995), p. 49. In 2012, Sibley was convicted of downloading more
than 13,000 indecent images of children onto his computer. He was given a
suspended jail sentence. Drawing on Sibleys' work here in no way condones
or excuses this behaviour, but nor is it satisfactory to ignore or deny his work,
which remains very influential.

16. E.V. Walter, 'Dreadful Enclosures: Detoxifying and Urban Myth', *European
Journal of Sociology* 18/1 (1977): 150–159, quote from p. 154.

17. L. Wacquant, 'Territorial Stigmatisation in the Age of Advanced Marginality',
Thesis Eleven 91/1 (2007): 66–77; see also, Wacquant, *Urban Outcasts: A
Comparative Sociology of Advanced Marginality* (Cambridge: Polity Press,
2008).

18. Wacquant, 'Territorial Stigmatisation', pp. 67–68.

19. L. Wacquant, T. Slater and V. Borges Pereira, 'Territorial Stigmatization in
Action', *Environment and Planning A* 46/6 (2014): 1270–1280.

20. P. Bourdieu, *Language and Symbolic Power* (Cambridge: Polity Press, 1979),
p. 79.

21. P. Bourdieu, *The Logic of Practice* (Cambridge: Polity Press, 1989), p. 138.

22. P. Bourdieu, 'Social Space and Symbolic Power', *Sociological Theory* 7/1
(1989): 14–25.

23. P. Bourdieu and L. Wacquant, *An Invitation to Reflexive Sociology* (Cambridge:
Polity Press, 1992), p. 167.

24. E. Said, *Orientalism* (London: Penguin, 2003), p. 54, original emphasis.

25. Ibid., p. 21, original emphasis.

26. Ibid., pp. 2–3.

27. Ibid., p. 5.

28. Ibid.

29. Ibid., p. 6.

30. R. Shields, *Places on the Margin: Alternative Geographies of Modernity*
(London: Routledge, 1991), p. 3.

31. Sibley, *Geographies of Exclusion*, p. 1.

32. Ibid.

33. Ibid., pp. 36–39.

34. Ibid., p. 2.

35. Ibid., p. 32.

36. G. Osborne, 'Speech to the Conservative Party Conference', 2012 (available at: http://www.newstatesman.com/blogs/politics/2012/10/george-osbornes-speech-conservative-conference-full-text, accessed 13 March 2017).
37. P. Bourdieu and L. Wacquant, *An Invitation to Reflexive Sociology* (Cambridge: Polity Press, 1992), p. 235, emphasis removed.
38. P. Bourdieu, *Sociology in Question* (Cambridge: Polity Press, 1993), p. 269.
39. P. DiMaggio, 'On Pierre Bourdieu', *American Journal of Sociology* 84/6 (1979): 1460–1474.
40. J. Painter, 'Pierre Bourdieu', in M. Crang and N. Thrift (eds), *Thinking Space* (London: Routledge, 2000), pp. 239–258.
41. P. Bourdieu, *On Television* (Cambridge: Polity Press, 2011), p. 17.
42. Bourdieu, 'Social Space and Symbolic Power', p. 16.
43. P. Bourdieu, *Outline of a Theory of Practice* (Cambridge: Cambridge University Press, 1977), pp. 159–171.
44. Bourdieu et al., *Weight of the World*, p. 123, original emphasis.
45. Ibid., original emphasis.
46. Ibid., p. 128.
47. E. Pickles, 'Speech to the National Conservation Convention', 5 April 2014 (available at: http://press.conservatives.com/post/82077378511/eric-pickles-speech-to-the-national-conservative, accessed 29 November 2016).
48. Bourdieu et al., *Weight of the World*, p. 181.
49. M. Edelman, *The Symbolic Uses of Politics* (Chicago: University of Illinois Press, 1964), p. 101.
50. R. Merrick, 'East Durham Schools "Smell of Defeatism" says Education Secretary, Michael Gove', *Northern Echo*, 1 March 2013 (available at: http://www.thenorthernecho.co.uk/news/10260028.East_Durham_schools__smell_of_defeatism__says_Education_Secretary__Michael_Gove/, accessed 13 March 2017).
51. Sibley, *Geographies of Exclusion*, p. 115.

CHAPTER 2

1. B. Disraeli, *Sybil, Or the Two Nations* [1845] (Oxford: Oxford University Press, 2017), p. 60.
2. E. Said, *Orientalism* (London: Penguin, 2003).
3. G. Mooney, '"Remoralizing" the Poor? Gender, Class and Philanthropy in Victorian England', in G. Lewis (ed.), *Forming Nation, Framing Welfare* (London: Routledge, 1998), pp. 49–92.
4. B. Anderson, *Imagined Communities: Reflections on the Origin and Spread of Nationalism* (London: Verso, 1983).
5. M. Harrington, *The Other America* (New York: Macmillian, 1963).
6. P. Bourdieu, J.-C. Chamboredon and J.-C. Passeron, *The Craft of Sociology: Epistemological Preliminaries* (New York: Walter de Gruyter, 1991), p. 20.
7. S. Koven, *Slumming: Sexual and Social Politics in Victorian London* (Princeton: Princeton University Press. 2004).

8. Kirk Mann notes the paradoxical situation of the 'racist ideology of imperialism' being used to describe the working classes who were then called upon to serve in the British army and protect the empire: K. Mann, *Making of an English Underclass? Social Divisions of Welfare and Labour* (Milton Keynes: Open University Press, 1992), p. 48.

9. Quoted in J.R. Walkowitz, *City of Dreadful Delight: Narratives of Sexual Danger in Late Victorian London* (Chicago: Chicago University Press, 1992), p. 19.

10. Koven, *Slumming*, p. 61.

11. Ibid., p. 237.

12. Toynbee Hall still exists and works to tackle poverty today. Its patron is HRH Princess Alexandra and its ambassadors include Dr John Sentamu, the archbishop of York, Jon Snow, the television news presenter, and Polly Toynbee, the *Guardian* columnist and author. Little has changed, although none of the above people live in Toynbee Hall.

13. Quoted in D. Weiner, *Architecture and Social Reform in Late-Victorian London* (Manchester: Manchester University Press, 1994), p. 8.

14. Ibid., p. 8.

15. Koven, *Slumming*, p. 61.

16. G. Sims, *How the Poor Live* (London: Chatto & Windus, 1883), p. 1.

17. W. Booth, *In Darkest England, and the Way Out* (London: Salvation Army, 1890).

18. Booth, *In Darkest England*, p. 9.

19. Ibid., p. 11.

20. Ibid., pp. 11–12.

21. Ibid., p. 14.

22. Ibid., p. 147.

23. Ibid., p. 156.

24. See 'William Branwell Booth, His Life and Ministry: A Very Short Biography' (available at: http://www.gospeltruth.net/booth/boothbioshort.htm, accessed 25 November 2016).

25. See e.g. J. Bierman, *Dark Safari: The Life Behind the Legend of Henry Morton Stanley* (New York: Knopf, 1990); and R. Lefort, 'Row over Statue of "Cruel" Explorer Henry Morton Stanley', *Daily Telegraph*, 25 July 2010 (available at: http://www.telegraph.co.uk/news/worldnews/africaandindianocean/congo/7908247/Row-over-statue-of-cruel-explorer-Henry-Morton-Stanley.html, accessed 14 March 2017).

26. Women's Group on Public Welfare, *Our Towns, a Close-Up: A Study Made During 1939–1942* (London: Oxford University Press, 1943).

27. Ibid., p. 102.

28. Oscar Lewis, *La Vida: A Puerto Rican Family in the Culture Of Poverty* (New York: Random House, 1965), p. 47.

29. Harrington, *The Other America*, p. 3.

30. Ibid., p. 6.

31. Ibid., p. 4.

32. Ibid., p. 10.

33. Ibid., p. 12.
34. Ibid.
35. Ibid., p. 65.
36. Ibid., p. 158.
37. Ibid.
38. Ibid., p. 161.
39. Ibid., p. 162.
40. See e.g. R. Lowe, 'The Rediscovery of Poverty and the Creation of the Child Poverty Action Group, 1962–68', *Contemporary British History* 9/3 (1995): 602–611.
41. See P. Townsend, *Poverty in the United Kingdom* (London: Penguin Books, 1979). The opening paragraph sets out possibly the most widely used and best-known definition of relative poverty: 'Poverty can be defined objectively and applied consistently only in terms of the concept of relative deprivation. That is the theme of this book. The term is understood objectively rather than subjectively. Individuals, families and groups in the population can be said to be in poverty when they lack the resources to obtain the types of diet, participate in the activities and have the living conditions and amenities which are customary, or are at least widely encouraged or approved, in the societies to which they belong. Their resources are so seriously below those commanded by the average individual or family that they are, in effect, excluded from ordinary living patterns, customs and activities' (ibid., p. 31).
42. H. Glennerster, J. Hills, D. Piachaud and J. Webb, 'One Hundred Years of Poverty and Policy (York: Joseph Rowntree Foundation, 2004).
43. T. Shildrick, R. Macdonald, C. Webster and K. Garthwaite, *Poverty and Insecurity: Life in Low-Pay, No-Pay Britain* (Bristol: Policy Press, 2012).
44. See T. Shildrick, R. MacDonald, A. Furlong, J. Roden and R. Crow, 'Are Cultures of Worklessness Passed Down the Generations?' (York: Joseph Rowntree Foundation, 2012).
45. C.A. Stabile and J. Morooka, 'Between Two Evils I Refuse to Choose the Lesser', *Cultural Studies* 17/3–4 (2003): 326–348.
46. Tony Blair, 'Beveridge Lecture', 18 March 1999 (available at: www.bristol. ac.uk/poverty/.../Tony%20Blair%20Child%20Poverty%20Speech.doc, accessed 14 March 2017).
47. 'Brown Unveils Child Poverty Targets', *BBC News*, 14 July 1999 (available at: http://news.bbc.co.uk/1/hi/uk_politics/394115.stm, accessed 26 November 2016).
48. R. Levitas, 'There May Be "Trouble" Ahead: What We Know about Those 120,000 "Troubled" Families', Policy Response Series No. 3, Poverty and Social Exclusion in the UK, 2012 (available at: http://www.poverty.ac.uk/system/files/WP%20Policy%20Response%20No.3-%20%20%27Trouble%27%20ahead%20(Levitas%20Final%2021April2012).pdf, accessed 13 March 2017).
49. Conservative Party Social Justice Policy Group, 'Breakdown Britain: Interim Report on the State of the Nation', Centre for Social Justice, 2006 (available at:

http://www.centreforsocialjustice.org.uk/core/wp-content/uploads/2016/08/
Breakdown-Britain.pdf , accessed 20 April 2017).

50. Centre for Social Justice (CSJ), 'Breakthrough Britain: Ending the
Costs of Social Breakdown: Overview', 2007 (available at: http://www.
centreforsocialjustice.org.uk/library/breakthrough-britain-chairmans-
overview , accessed 20 April 2017).

51. CSJ, 'Breakthrough Britain', p. 5.

52. D. Hencke, P. Wintour and H. Mulholland, 'Cameron Launches Tory "Broken
Society Byelection" Campaign', *Guardian*, 7 July 2008 (available at: https://
www.theguardian.com/politics/2008/jul/07/davidcameron.conservatives,
accessed 14 March 2017).

53. Cameron and Brooks were part of the 'Chipping Norton set', a group of
political, media and journalistic friends who gained notoriety in the wake of
the News International phone-hacking scandal.

54. G. Pascoe-Watson, 'David Cameron: Tory Leader Plans to Mend Broken
Britain', *Sun*, 15 January 2008, p. 8.

55. See e.g. press releases from the CSJ such as 'Benefit Ghettos of Britain Exposed
by CSJ in Major New Inquiry into Welfare State', 19 May 2013 (available at:
http://www.centreforsocialjustice.org.uk/press-releases/benefit-ghettos-of-
britain-exposed-by-csj-in-major-new-inquiry-into-welfare-state, accessed
27 November 2016); 'Seaside Towns Becoming "Dumping Grounds" for
Vulnerable as Benefits Bill Nears £2 Billion', 5 August 2013 (available at: http://
www.centreforsocialjustice.org.uk/press-releases/seaside-towns-becoming-
dumping-grounds-for-vulnerable-as-benefits-bill-nears-2-billion, accessed
27 November 2016); and 'Lone Parents Tally Heads for Two Million as
Numbers Rise 20,000 a Year, Says CSJ Report', 10 June 2013 (available at:
http://www.centreforsocialjustice.org.uk/press-releases/lone-parents-tally-
heads-for-two-million-as-numbers-rise-20000-a-year-says-csj-report,
accessed 27 November 2016).

56. CSJ, 'Transforming Lives to Strengthen Britain: A Social Justice Manifesto
for 2015', 2015 (available at: http://www.centreforsocialjustice.org.uk/library/
transforming-lives-strengthen-britain-social-justice-manifesto-2015,
accessed 14 March 2017), p. 5.

57. For a fuller examination of the response from these three individuals, see
S. Crossley and T. Slater, 'Benefits Street: Territorial Stigmatisation and the
Realization of a '(Tele)Vision of Divisions', 2014 (available at: https://values.
doc.gold.ac.uk/blog/18/, accessed 22 January 2017).

58. F. Nelson, '*Benefits Street* Exposes Britain's Dirty Secret – How
Welfare Imprisons The Poor', *Spectator*, 18 January 2014 (available at:
http://www.spectator.co.uk/features/9116701/britains-dirty-secret/, accessed
7 August 2014).

59. Ibid.

60. Ibid.

61. Ibid.

62. 'Benefits Street Reaction Shows Poor "Ghettoised", says Duncan Smith', BBC News, 23 January 2014 (available at: http://www.bbc.co.uk/news/uk-politics-25866259, accessed 27 November 2016).

63. Ibid.

64. C. Guy, 'Don't Pretend Benefits Street is Fiction', Huffington Post, 28 January 2014 (available at: http://www.huffingtonpost.co.uk/christian-guy-/benefits-street_b_4674070.html, accessed 14 February 2014).

65. Ibid.

66. Baroness Grender, Speech during House of Lords debate, 6 November 2014 (available at: https://www.theyworkforyou.com/lords/?id=2014-11-06a.1774.0, accessed 27 November 2016).

67. S. Crossley, 'The Troubled Families Programme: The Perfect Social Policy?' Centre from Crime and Justice Studies, 2015 (available at: https://www.crimeandjustice.org.uk/publications/troubled-families-programme-perfect-social-policy, accessed 17 March 2017).

68. J. Lyons, 'Liberal Democrat Peer: We Struggle to Get By on £300 Per Day Tax-Free Allowance', Daily Mirror, 3 October 2014 (available at: http://www.mirror.co.uk/news/uk-news/liberal-democrat-peer-struggle-300-4370228, accessed 14 March 2017).

69. Rob Williams, 'Poor "Live Like Animals" Says Boris's Privately Educated Sister after Going on "Poverty Safari"', Independent, 5 March 2014 (available at: http://www.independent.co.uk/news/uk/home-news/poor-live-like-animals-says-boriss-privately-educated-sister-after-going-on-poverty-safari-9170440.html, accessed 27 November 2016).

70. Ibid.

71. R. Johnson, 'Don't Get Angry at My "Poverty Safari" – Be Outraged that People Go Hungry', Mail on Sunday, 9 March 2014 (available at: http://www.dailymail.co.uk/debate/article-2576614/RACHEL-JOHNSON-Dont-angry-poverty-safari-outraged-people-hungry.html#ixzz4RCqpYKua, accessed 27 November 2016).

72. Sibley, Geographies of Exclusion, p. 51.

73. E. Jackson and M. Benson, 'Neither "Deepest, Darkest Peckham" nor "Run-of-the-Mill" East Dulwich: The Middle Classes and their "Others" in an Inner-London Neighbourhood', International Journal of Urban and Regional Research 38/4 (2014): 1195–1210.

74. M. Buerk, 'Boris Johnson's Sister Rachel: I Was So Precious, So Spoilt', Radio Times, 12 March 2014 (available at: http://www.radiotimes.com/news/2014-03-12/boris-johnsons-sister-rachel-i-was-so-precious-so-spoilt, accessed 14 March 2017).

75. In the US state of Georgia, the charity Habitat for Humanity have developed the Global Village and Discovery Centre where people can 'visit the world' in one place. This includes a 'Living in Poverty' area where in a 'life-sized representation of some of the world's worst examples of poverty housing, you can experience first-hand the living conditions poor people must battle' and where visitors can 'imagine living in a structure where it's impossible to secure your possessions or protect your family against intruders'

(http://www.habitat.org/about/global-village-discovery-center, accessed 27 November 2016).
76. Walkowitz, *City of Dreadful Delight*, p. 16.

CHAPTER 3

1. R. Shields, *Places on the Margin: Alternative Geographies of Modernity* (London: Routledge, 1991), p. 3.
2. S. Lawler, 'White Like Them: Whiteness and Anachronistic Space in Representations of the English White Working Class', *Ethnicities* 12/4 (2012): 409–426.
3. J. Temple, 'Detroit: The Last Days', *Guardian*, 10 March 2010 (available at: https://www.theguardian.com/film/2010/mar/10/detroit-motor-city-urban-decline, accessed 27 November 2017).
4. J.P. Leary, 'Detroitism', *Guernica*, 15 January 2011 (available at: https://www.guernicamag.com/features/leary_1_15_11/, accessed 27 November 2016).
5. A. Moore, *Detroit Disassembled* (Bologna: Damiani, 2010); Y. Marchand and R. Meffre, *The Ruins of Detroit* (Gottingen: Steidl, 2010).
6. Leary, 'Detroitism'.
7. 'Tyler Fernengel BMX Session: Silverdome', 9 July 2015' (available at: https://www.youtube.com/watch?v=XpmEaSi5YNw, accessed 26 November 2016).
8. 'New Ski Film: Tracing Skylines', 20 August 2013 (available at: http://www.redbull.com/us/en/snow/stories/1331604657621/tracing-skylines, accessed 27 November 2016).
9. Jonny Joo, 'Architectural Afterlife: Preserving Our Almost Lost History' (available at: https://architecturalafterlife.com/, accessed 27 November 2016).
10. 'The Pontiac Silverdome's Final Moments', 30 October 2015 (available at: https://architecturalafterlife.com/2015/10/30/the-pontiac-silverdomes-final-moments/, accessed 27 November 2016).
11. B. Doucet and D. Philp, 'In Detroit "Ruin Porn" Ignores the Voices of Those Who Still Call the City Home', *Guardian*, 15 February 2016 (available at: https://www.theguardian.com/housing-network/2016/feb/15/ruin-porn-detroit-photography-city-homes, accessed 27 November 2016).
12. For a powerful and compelling alternative photographic account of Detroit, which places its residents centre stage, see D. Jordano, *Detroit: Unbroken Down* (New York: Powerhouse Books, 2015).
13. D. Sibley, *Geographies of Exclusion: Society and Difference in the West* (London: Routledge, 1995), p. 26.
14. K. Abbey-Lambertz, 'Detroit's Abandoned Ruins Are Captivating, but Are They Bad for Neighbourhoods?' *Huffington Post*, 30 December 2013 (available at: http://www.huffingtonpost.com/2013/12/30/detroit-ruins_n_4519731.html, accessed 27 November 2016).
15. 'Pontiac Silverdome's Final Moments'.
16. Leary, 'Detroitism'.
17. Ibid.

18. Temple, 'Detroit'.
19. T. Shildrick, R. Macdonald, C. Webster and K. Garthwaite, *Poverty and Insecurity: Life in Low-Pay, No-Pay Britain* (Bristol: Policy Press, 2012), p. 40.
20. S. Dalton, 'Blade Runner: Anatomy of a Classic', 26 October 2016 (available at: http://www.bfi.org.uk/news-opinion/news-bfi/features/blade-runner, accessed 17 January 2017).
21. L. Thomas Jr., 'A Faded Industrial Town Is Feeling Britain's Cuts', *New York Times*, 17 March 2011 (available at: http://www.nytimes.com/2011/03/18/business/global/18welfare.html, accessed 14 March 2017).
22. M. Goldfarb, 'In England, a Shrinking Middle Class Struggles to Hold On', *Alaska Dispatch News*, 4 February 2013 (available at: https://www.adn.com/nation-world/article/englands-shrinking-middle-class-struggles-hold/2013/02/05/, accessed 27 November 2016).
23. A. Beckett, 'The North-East of England: Britain's Detroit?' *Guardian*, 10 May 2014 (available at: https://www.theguardian.com/uk-news/2014/may/10/north-east-avoid-becoming-britains-detroit, accessed 27 November 2016).
24. Shields, *Places on the Margin*, p. 3.
25. H. Pearson, *The Far Corner: A Mazy Dribble through North-East Football* (London: Little, Brown, 1994).
26. Beckett, 'North-East of England'.
27. Ibid.
28. Women's Group on Public Welfare, *Our Towns, a Close-Up: A Study Made During 1939–1942* (London: Oxford University Press, 1943).
29. Beckett, 'North-East of England'.
30. T. Leunig and J. Swaffield, 'Cities Unlimited: Making Urban Regeneration Work', Policy Exchange, 2007 (available at: https://www.policyexchange.org.uk/wp-content/uploads/2016/09/cities-unlimited-aug-08.pdf, accessed 14 March 2017), p. 31.
31. Ibid., p. 5.
32. Ibid.
33. P. Bourdieu et al., *The Weight of the World: Social Suffering in Contemporary Society* (Cambridge: Polity Press, 1999), p. 627.
34. Ibid., p. 627.
35. L. Borromeo, 'These Anti-Homeless Spikes Are Brutal. We Need to Get Rid of Them', *Guardian*, 23 July 2015 (available at: https://www.thcguardian.com/commentisfree/2015/jul/23/anti-homeless-spikes-inhumane-defensive-architecture, accessed 27 November 2016).
36. 'Camden Bench', Factory Furniture (available at: http://www.factoryfurniture.co.uk/camden-bench/, accessed 27 November 2016).
37. R. Atkinson and A. White, 'Defensive Architecture: Designing the Homeless out of Cities', *The Conversation*, 30 December 2015 (available at: https://theconversation.com/defensive-architecture-designing-the-homeless-out-of-cities-52399, accessed 27 November 2016).
38. See G. Mooney, K. Paton and V. McCall, 'Behind the Fence: The Side of Glasgow Games You're Not Meant to See', *The Conversation*, 30 July 2014 (available at: https://theconversation.com/behind-the-fence-the-side-of-

glasgow-games-youre-not-meant-to-see-29927, accessed 27 November 2016). Mooney, Paton and McCall have, in a series of pieces examining the impact of the Commonwealth Games on communities in the East End of Glasgow, skilfully highlighted the need to reinsert spatial analyses into attempts to understand contemporary class dynamics in the UK. They document the houses that were demolished and the facilities and services that were closed or had access arrangements changed to make way for the infrastructure of the games.

39. 'Glasgow 2014: Red Road Flats Demolition Dropped from Opening', BBC News, 13 April 2014 (available at: http://www.bbc.co.uk/news/uk-scotland-glasgow-west-27009806, accessed 27 November 2016).

40. Mooney et al., 'Behind the Fence'.

41. B. Hughes, Review of From Moorepark to 'Wine Alley': The Rise and Fall of a Glasgow Housing Estate', Critical Social Policy 10/28 (1990): 122–124.

42. A. Schwartz, 'The "Poor Door" and the Glossy Reconfiguration of City Life', New Yorker, 22 January 2016 (available at: http://www.newyorker.com/culture/cultural-comment/the-poor-door-and-the-glossy-reconfiguration-of-city-life, accessed 14 March 2017).

43. H. Osborne, 'Poor Doors: The Segregation of London's Inner-City Flat Dwellers', Guardian, 25 July 2014 (available at: https://www.theguardian.com/society/2014/jul/25/poor-doors-segregation-london-flats, accessed 27 November 2016).

44. S.W. Davies, 'What's My Weekend: Taylor McWilliams, Housekeeping', Elle, 2 May 2014 (available at: http://www.elleuk.com/life-and-culture/travel/articles/a21634/what-s-my-weekend-taylor-mcwilliams-housekeeping/, accessed 27 November 2016).

45. Anti-Social Behaviour, Crime and Policing Act 2014, pt. 1, sec. 2.

46. B.L. Garrett, 'PSPOs: The New Control Orders Threatening Our Public Spaces, Guardian, 8 September 2015 (available at: https://www.theguardian.com/cities/2015/sep/08/pspos-new-control-orders-public-spaces-asbos-freedoms, accessed 27 November 2016).

47. 'No Need to Beg', Newcastle City Council, 23 November 2015 (available at: https://www.newcastle.gov.uk/news-story/no-need-beg, accessed 27 November 2016).

48. J. Appleton, 'PSPOs: A Busybodies' Charter', Manifesto Club, 29 February 2016 (available at: http://manifestoclub.info/psposreport/, accessed 27 November 2016).

49. 'ASB Dispersal Powers: The Crime of Being Found in a Public Place', Manifesto Club, 13 November 2014 (available at: http://manifestoclub.info/asb-dispersal-powers-the-crime-of-being-found-in-a-public-place/, accessed 27 November 2016).

50. Shields, Places on the Margin, p. 3.

51. W. Morris, Signs of Change [1888] (available at: https://www.marxists.org/archive/morris/works/1888/signs/signs.htm, accessed 27 November 2016).

52. W. Morris, 'How I Became a Socialist' [1894] (available at: https://www.marxists.org/archive/morris/works/1894/hibs/hibs.htm, accessed 27 November 2016).

53. Landon Thomas Jr. was reported by the local newspaper, the *Evening Gazette* to have taken afternoon tea with the Middlesbrough mayor, Ray Mallon, on his visit to the town for his *New York Times* article. See 'Middlesbrough Hits Back at New York Times', 23 May 2013 (available at: http://www.gazettelive.co.uk/news/local-news/middlesbrough-hits-back-new-york-3684946, accessed 20 April 2017).

CHAPTER 4

1. E.V. Walter, 'Dreadful Enclosures: Detoxifying and Urban Myth', *European Journal of Sociology* 18/1 (1977): 150–159, quote from p. 155.

2. Bowley, along with his colleague A.R. Bennett Hurst, conducted research in four towns in the 1910s, the results published as *Livelihood and Poverty: A Study in the Economic Conditions of Working-Class Households* (London: G. Bell and Sons, 1915). Bowley is widely credited with developing the methodological innovation of sampling techniques and, in 1919, was appointed to the newly created chair of statistics at the London School of Economics.

3. S. Koven, *Slumming: Sexual and Social Politics in Victorian London* (Princeton: Princeton University Press. 2004), p. 8.

4. M. Harrington, *The Other America* (New York: Macmillian, 1963).

5. 'Poverty Tour Brought LBJ to NC', *News and Observer* (Raleigh, NC), 2 May 2014 (available at: http://www.newsobserver.com/living/liv-columns-blogs/past-times/article10325423.html, accessed 27 November 2016).

6. D. Cameron, 'Estate Regeneration', 10 January 2016 (available at: https://www.gov.uk/government/speeches/estate-regeneration-article-by-david-cameron, accessed 27 November 2016). All quotes in this and the next paragraph are taken from this source.

7. D. Boffey, 'David Cameron's £140m to Tear Down Sink Estates Turns Out to Be a Loan', *Observer*, 27 February 2016, https://www.theguardian.com/society/2016/feb/27/david-cameron-sink-estates-fund-turns-out-to-be-loan, accessed 27 November 2016).

8. H. Hariss, 'Bulldozing Brutalism's Bad Boys to Balance the Books Won't Work', *Architect's Journal*, 18 January 2016 (available at: https://www.architectsjournal.co.uk/opinion/bulldozing-brutalisms-bad-boys-to-balance-the-books-wont-work/10001687.article?blocktitle=Opinion&contentID=13629, accessed 27 November 2016).

9. L. Hanley, 'Cameron Cannot 'Blitz' Poverty by Bulldozing Housing Estates', *Guardian*, 19 January 2016 (available at: https://www.theguardian.com/society/2016/jan/19/cameron-poverty-bulldozing-housing-estates, accessed 27 November 2016).

10. R. Lupton, '"Neighbourhood Effects": Can We Measure Them and Does It Matter?' CASE paper No. 73, Centre for Analysis of Social Exclusion, London

School of Economics and Political Science, 2003 (available at: http://eprints.
lse.ac.uk/6327/1/Neighbourhood_Effects_Can_we_measure_them_and_
does_it_matter.pdf, accessed 15 March 2017).

11. H. Bauder, 'Neighbourhood Effects and Cultural Exclusion', *Urban Studies*
    39/1 (2002): 85–93.

12. T. Slater, 'Your Life Chances Affect Where You Live: A Critique of the
    "Cottage Industry" of Neighbourhood Effects Research', *International Journal
    of Urban and Regional Research* 37/2 (2013): 367–387.

13. Ibid., original emphasis.

14. L. Wacquant, 'Territorial Stigmatisation in the Age of Advanced Marginality',
    Thesis Eleven 91/1 (2007): 66–77.

15. Ibid., p. 67.

16. See the special issue of *Environment and Planning A* 46/6 (2014) for
    discussions of territorial stigmatisation in different countries and contexts.

17. 'Denmark Has Fewer Ghettos This Year', *CPH Post*, 1 December 2014
    (available at: http://cphpost.dk/news/denmark-has-fewer-ghettos-this-year.
    html, accessed 27 November 2016).

18. Wacquant, 'Territorial Stigmatization', p. 68.

19. L. Wacquant, T. Slater and V. Borges Pereira, 'Territorial Stigmatization in
    Action', *Environment and Planning A* 46/6 (2014): 1270–1280, quote from p.
    1273.

20. R. Lupton and A. Fitzgerald, 'The Coalition's Record on Area Regeneration
    and Neighbourhood Renewal 2010–2015', Working Paper No. 19, Social
    Policy in a Cold Climate, 2015 (available at: http://sticerd.lse.ac.uk/dps/case/
    spcc/wp19.pdf, accessed 27 November 2016).

21. L. Hanley, *Estates: An Intimate History* (London: Granta, 2007); L. McKenzie,
    Getting By: Estates, Class and Culture in Austerity Britain (Bristol: Policy
    Press, 2015).

22. M. Fletcher, 'Demolition of the Aylesbury Estate: A New Dawn for Hell's
    Waiting Room?' *The Times*, 20 October 2008 (available at: http://www.
    thetimes.co.uk/article/demolition-of-the-aylesbury-estate-a-new-dawn-for-
    hells-waiting-room-jglhxhw396s, accessed 15 March 2017).

23. Ibid.

24. Ibid.

25. P. Vallely, 'He Visited in Glory Days of '97, but Has Blair Kept His Vow
    to Aylesbury Estate?' *Independent*, 11 April 2005 (available at: http://www.
    independent.co.uk/news/uk/politics/he-visited-in-glory-days-of-97-but-
    has-blair-kept-his-vow-to-aylesbury-estate-484821.html, accessed 27
    November 2016).

26. T. Blair, 'Aylesbury Estate Speech', 2 June 1997 (available at: https://web.
    archive.org/web/20070626045507/http://archive.cabinetoffice.gov.uk/seu/
    newsa52f.html?id=400, accessed 27 November 2016). All remaining quotes
    in this paragraph are taken from this source.

27. M. Edelman, *The Symbolic Uses of Politics* (Chicago: University of Illinois
    Press, 1964), p. 95.

28. 'How Iain Duncan Smith Came to Easterhouse and Left with a New Vision for the Tory Party', *Herald Scotland*, 23 March 2002 (available at: http://www. heraldscotland.com/news/12131837.How_Iain_Duncan_Smith_came_to_ Easterhouse_and_left_with_a_new_vision_for_the_Tory_party/, accessed 27 November 2016).

29. J. Derbyshire, 'Poor Relations', *New Statesman*, 1 March 2010 (available at: http://www.newstatesman.com/uk-politics/2010/03/duncan-smith-social-interview, accessed 27 November 2016).

30. P. Goodman, 'IDS, Today's Wilberforce', *Conservative Home*, 3 January 2013 (available at: http://www.conservativehome.com/thetorydiary/2013/01/ids. html, accessed 27 November 2016).

31. B. Anderson, 'This Welfare Revolution Could Hinge on a Single Word: Fairness', *Daily Telegraph*, 31 March 2013 (available at: http://www.telegraph. co.uk/news/politics/conservative/9964420/This-welfare-revolution-could-hinge-on-a-single-word-fairness.html, accessed 27 November 2016).

32. Goodman, 'IDS'.

33. B. Holman, 'I Thought I Knew Iain Duncan Smith', *Guardian*, 12 November 2010 (available at: https://www.theguardian.com/commentisfree/2010/ nov/12/iain-duncan-smith-punishing-the-poor, accessed 27 November 2016).

34. L. Martin, 'Mother Who Changed IDS Forever', *Guardian*, 26 November 2006 (available at: https://www.theguardian.com/society/2006/nov/26/ drugsandalcohol.politics, accessed 27 November 2016).

35. Anderson, 'welfare revolution'.

36. Centre for Social Justice, 'Breakthrough Glasgow: Ending the Costs of Social Breakdown', 2008 (available at: http://www.centreforsocialjustice.org.uk/ library/breakthrough-glasgow, accessed 24 March 2017), p. 7.

37. Derbyshire, 'Poor Relations'.

38. P. Bourdieu, 'Social Space and Symbolic Power', *Sociological Theory* 7/1 (1989): 14–25, quote from p. 16.

39. Ibid., p. 16.

40. M. Hughes, 'Whatever Happened to the Hoodie Cameron Told Us to Hug?' *Independent*, 13 April 2010 (available at: http://www.independent.co.uk/ news/uk/politics/whatever-happened-to-the-hoodie-cameron-told-us-to-hug-1944065.html, accessed 27 November 2016).

41. P. Bourdieu et al., *The Weight of the World: Social Suffering in Contemporary Society* (Cambridge: Polity Press, 1999), p. 123.

42. See e.g. C. Beatty and S. Fothergill, 'The Uneven Impact of Welfare Reform: The Financial Losses to Places and People', Centre for Regional Economic and Social Research, Sheffield Hallam University, 2016 (available at: http:// www4.shu.ac.uk/research/cresr/sites/shu.ac.uk/files/welfare-reform-2016. pdf, accessed 15 March 2017).

43. D. Innes and G. Tetlow, 'Central Cuts, Local Decision-Making: Changes in Local Government Spending and Revenues in England, 2009–10 to 2014–15', IFS Briefing Note BN166, Institute for Fiscal Studies, 2015 (available at:

https://www.ifs.org.uk/uploads/publications/bns/BN166.pdf, accessed 15
March 2017).

44. S. Weale, 'Thousands of Schools Stand to Lose Out under New Funding
Formula', *Guardian*, 14 December 2016 (available at: https://www.
theguardian.com/politics/2016/dec/14/england-school-funding-formula-
justine-greening-education-secretary, accessed 18 January 2017).

CHAPTER 5

1. 'Our London Letter', *Advertiser*, 14 November 1910 (available at: http://trove.
nla.gov.au/newspaper/article/5208971, accessed 20 April 2017).
2. E. Brodkin, 'Putting Street-Level Organizations First: New Directions for
Social Policy and Management Research', *Journal of Public Administration
Research and Theory* 21/S2 (2011): 191–201, quotes from pp. 199–201.
3. Ibid., p. 200.
4. C. Geertz, 'Thick Description: Toward an Interpretive Theory of Culture', in
The Interpretation of Cultures: Selected Essays (New York: Basic Books, 1973),
pp. 3–30.
5. Ibid., p. 21.
6. Ibid., p. 23.
7. Ibid., p. 22.
8. Ibid., p. 23.
9. See e.g. L. Wacquant, 'Thick Construction: Theory, Body and Social
Relations in Ethnography', lecture given at the School of Architecture
and Urban Planning and School of Social Science, Universidad de Chile,
Santiago, Chile, 15 October 2013; and L. Wacquant, 'The Science and Craft
of Thick Construction', keynote address at the conference 'Governing Urban
Marginality', Sheffield Hallam University, Sheffield, 8 June 2016.
10. N. Anderson, *The Hobo: The Sociology of the Homeless Man* (Chicago:
University of Chicago Press, 1923); W.I. Thomas, *The Unadjusted Girl, with
Cases and Standpoint for Behaviour Analysis* (Boston: Little, Brown, 1923);
Frederick Thrasher, *The Gang: A Study of 1,313 Gangs in Chicago* (Chicago:
University of Chicago Press, 1927).
11. William Foote Whyte, *Street Corner Society* (Chicago: University of Chicago
Press, 1943).
12. Ibid., p. xv.
13. Ibid.
14. E. Anderson, *A Place on the Corner* (Chicago: University of Chicago
Press, 1976); E. Anderson, *Streetwise: Race, Class and Change in an Urban
Community* (Chicago: University of Chicago Press, 1990); E. Anderson, *Code
of the Street: Decency, Violence, and the Moral Life of the Inner City* (New York:
Norton, 2000).
15. Anderson, *Streetwise*, p. ix.
16. Ibid., pp. 5–6.
17. Ibid.
18. Ibid., p. 210.

19. Ibid., pp. 3–5.
20. Anderson, *Code of the Street*, p. 37.
21. Ibid., p. 38.
22. Ibid., p. 45.
23. Ibid., pp. 46–47.
24. Ibid., pp. 45–46.
25. L. Wacquant, 'Scrutinizing the Street: Poverty, Morality, and the Pitfalls of Urban Ethnography', *American Journal of Sociology* 107/6 (2002): 1468–1532.
26. See e.g. E. Lemert, *Social Pathology: A Systematic Approach to the Theory of Sociopathic Behaviour* (New York: McGraw-Hill, 1951); H. Becker, *Outsiders: Studies in the Sociology of Deviance* (New York: Free Press, 1963); D. Matza, *On Becoming Deviant* (Englewood Cliffs, NJ: Prentice Hall, 1969); S. Cohen, *Folk Devils and Moral Panics* (London: MacGibbon and Kee, 1972).
27. S. Sandberg, *Street Capital: Black Cannabis Dealers in a White Welfare State* (Bristol: Policy Press, 2009).
28. See S. Harding, *The Street Casino: Survival in Violent Street Gangs* (Bristol: Policy Press, 2014); and S. Harding, 'Street Government: The Role of the Urban Street Gang in the London Riots', in D. Briggs (ed.), *The English Riots of 2011: A Summer of Discontent* (Hook: Waterside Press, 2012), pp. 193–214.
29. Harding, *Street Casino*, p. 1.
30. Harding, 'Street Government', p. 193.
31. Ibid.
32. D. Cameron, 'Estate Regeneration', 10 January 2016 (available at: https://www.gov.uk/government/speeches/estate-regeneration-article-by-david-cameron, accessed 27 November 2016).
33. L. Wacquant, *Urban Outcasts: A Comparative Sociology of Advanced Marginality* (Cambridge: Polity Press, 2008).
34. C. Lemert, 'Foreword', in E. Liebow, *Tally's Corner: A Study of Negro Streetcorner Men* [1967], rev. edn (Lanham, MD: Rowman and Littlefield, 2003), pp. vii–xxvi, quote from p. xxiv, emphasis added.
35. Liebow, *Tally's Corner*, p. 6.
36. Ibid.
37. Ibid.
38. Ibid., p. 13.
39. Ibid., p. 11.
40. Ibid., p. 19.
41. Ibid., pp. 36–37.
42. Ibid., p. 136.
43. Ibid.
44. See e.g. T. Shildrick and R. Macdonald, 'Street Corner Society: Leisure Careers, Youth (Sub)Culture and Social Exclusion', *Leisure Studies* 26/3 (2007): 339–355.
45. R. Macdonald and J. Marsh, *Disconnected Youth? Growing Up in Britain's Poor Neighbourhoods* (Basingstoke: Palgrave, 2005), pp. 68–84.
46. O. Gill, *Luke Street: Housing Policy, Conflict and the Creation of the Delinquent Area* (London: Macmillan, 1977).

47. Ibid., p. ix.
48. Ibid., p. 110.
49. Ibid., p. 68.
50. L. McKenzie, *Getting By: Estates, Class and Culture in Austerity Britain* (Bristol: Policy Press, 2015).
51. Ibid., p. 164.
52. Ibid., p. 51.
53. Ibid.
54. A. Fraser, 'Street Habitus: Gangs, Territorialism and Social Change in Glasgow', *Journal of Youth Studies* 16/8 (2013): 970–985.

CHAPTER 6

1. Women's Group of Public Welfare, *Our Towns, a Close-Up: A Study Made During 1939–1942* (London: Oxford University Press, 1943), p. 10.
2. See e.g. P. Garrett, '"Sinbin" Solutions: The "Pioneer" Projects for "Problem Families" and the Forgetfulness of Social Policy Research', *Critical Social Policy* 27/2 (2007): 203–230; and J. Welshman, 'Recuperation, Rehabilitation and the Residential Option: The Brentwood Centre for Mothers and Children', *Twentieth Century British History* 19/4 (2008): 502–529.
3. Office for National Statistics (ONS), 'Households below Average Income: 1994/95 to 2014/15', 28 June 2016 (available at: https://www.gov.uk/government/statistics/households-below-average-income-199495-to-201415, accessed 30 November 2011).
4. R. Joyce, 'Child Poverty in Britain: Recent Trends and Future Prospects', IFS Working Paper W15/07, Institute for Fiscal Studies, 13 February 2015 (available at: https://www.ifs.org.uk/uploads/publications/wps/WP201507.pdf, accessed 16 March 2017).
5. ONS, 'Households below Average Income'.
6. See e.g. M. Young, 'Distribution of Income within the Family', *British Journal of Sociology* 3/4 (1952): 305–321.
7. Quoted in H. Land, 'Poverty and Gender: The Distribution of Resources within the Family', in M. Brown (ed.), *The Structure of Disadvantage* (London: Heinemann, 1983), pp. 49–71.
8. J. Goode, C. Callender and R. Lister, 'Purse or Wallet? Gender Inequalities and Income Distribution within Families on Benefits' (London: Policy Studies Institute, 1998).
9. Quoted in Land, 'Poverty and Gender', p. 60.
10. Ibid.
11. J. Brown, 'Pupils' Hunger "Worse in School Holidays"', *BBC News*, 5 April 2016 (available at: http://www.bbc.co.uk/news/education-35937343, accessed 30 November 2016).
12. C. Warburton-Brown, 'How Does Mum Manage? Investigating the Financial Circumstances of Mothers in Lower Income Working Families', PhD thesis, School of Political and Social Sciences, University of Glasgow (available at: http://theses.gla.ac.uk/2593/, accessed 30 November 2016).

13. Ibid., pp. 2–3.

14. Ibid., p. 10.

15. K. Hamilton, 'Low-Income Families and Coping through Brands: Inclusion or Stigma?' *Sociology* 46/1 (2012): 74–90.

16. Women's Group of Public Welfare, *Our Towns*, p. 9.

17. See e.g. Centre for Social Justice (CSJ), 'Breakthrough Britain: Family Breakdown', 2007 (available at: http://www.centreforsocialjustice.org.uk/ library/breakthrough-britain-family-breakdown, accessed 16 March 2017); CSJ, 'Forgotten Families? The Vanishing Agenda', 2012 (available at: http:// www.centreforsocialjustice.org.uk/library/forgotten-families-vanishing- agenda, accessed 16 March 2017); and CSJ, 'Fractured Families: Why Stability Matters, 2013 (available at: http://www.centreforsocialjustice.org.uk/library/ fractured-families-stability-matters, accessed 16 March 2017).

18. See e.g. S. McLanahan, 'Fragile Families and the Reproduction of Poverty', *Annals of the American Academy of Political and Social Science* 621/1 (2009): 111–131; and I. Garfinkel and A. Zilanawala, 'Fragile Families in the American Welfare State', *Children and Youth Services Review* 55 (2015): 210–221.

19. For the worst example, see the front-page headline '4m Scrounging Families in the UK', *Daily Express*, 2 September 2011, p. 1.

20. ONS, 'Statistical Bulletin: Working and Workless Households in the UK: Apr to June 2016' (available at: https://www.ons.gov.uk/ employmentandlabourmarket/peopleinwork/employmentand employeetypes/bulletins/workingandworklesshouseholds/aprtojune2016, accessed 30 November 2016), p. 5.

21. Tony Blair, 'Beveridge Lecture', 18 March 1999 (available at: www.bristol. ac.uk/poverty/.../Tony%20Blair%20Child%20Poverty%20Speech.doc, accessed 14 March 2017).

22. Child Poverty Act 2010, pt. 1, sec 1.

23. Ibid., pt. 1, sec. 7.

24. Joint Committee on Human Rights, 'Legislative Scrutiny: Child Poverty Bill Twenty-Eighth Report of Session 2008–2009' (available at: www.publications. parliament.uk/pa/jt200809/jtselect/jtrights/183/183.pdf [Accessed 30 November 2016), pp. 18–19.

25. R. Carr-Hill, 'Non-Household Populations: Implications for Measurements of Poverty Globally and in the UK', *Journal of Social Policy* 44/2 (2015): 255–275.

26. Ibid., p. 268.

27. Work and Welfare Reform Act 2016, pt. 1, sec. 3.

28. Ibid., pt. 1, sec. 5.

29. L. Elliott, 'Number of Children in Workless Households Hits Record Low', *Guardian*, 1 September 2016 (available at: https://www.theguardian.com/ uk-news/2016/sep/01/number-children-living-workless-households-hits- record-low-ons, accessed 30 November 2016).

30. F. McGuinness, 'Poverty in the UK: Statistics', House of Commons Library Briefing Paper No. 7096, 14 November 2016 (available at:

http://researchbriefings.parliament.uk/ResearchBriefing/Summary/
SN07096#fullreport, accessed 16 March 2017), p. 5.

31. Department for Communities and Local Government, 'National Evaluation
    of the Troubled Families Programme: National Impact Study Report', 2016
    (available at: https://www.gov.uk/government/uploads/system/uploads/
    attachment_data/file/560504/Troubled_Families_Evaluation_National_
    Impact_Study.pdf, accessed 16 March 2017), p. 144.

32. S. Crossley, 'The Troubled Families Programme: The Perfect Social Policy?'
    Briefing 13, Centre for Crime and Justice Studies, November 2015 (available
    at: https://www.crimeandjustice.org.uk/publications/troubled-families-
    programme-perfect-social-policy, accessed 17 March 2017).

33. J. Millar and C. Glendinning, 'Gender and Poverty', *Journal of Social Policy*
    18/3 (1989): 363–381.

34. Ibid., p. 363.

35. See e.g. J. Pahl, 'The Allocation of Money and the Structuring of Inequality
    within Marriage', *Sociological Review* 31/2 (1983): 237–262; and J. Pahl,
    Money and Marriage (London: Macmillan, 1989).

36. Department for Work and Pensions, 'Universal Credit: Welfare that Works',
    2010 (available at: https://www.gov.uk/government/uploads/system/uploads/
    attachment_data/file/48897/universal-credit-full-document.pdf, accessed 16
    March 2017).

37. Ibid., p. 34.

38. See e.g. V. Finnan, 'Benefits Cap to Be Slashed from £26,000 to £20,000
    Per Family: Claimants Told "Find Jobs or Your Handouts Will Be Cut"',
    Daily Mail, 7 May 2016 (available at: http://www.dailymail.co.uk/news/
    article-3578279/Benefits-cap-slashed-26-000-20-000-family-Claimants-
    told-jobs-handouts-cut.html, accessed 30 November 2016).

39. H. Stewart and S. Butler, 'Damian Green Says Government's Benefits Cap
    Is a "Real Success"', *Guardian*, 7 November 2016 (available at: https://www.
    theguardian.com/politics/2016/nov/07/damian-green-says-governments-
    benefits-cap-is-a-real-success, accessed 30 November 2016).

40. I. Duncan Smith, 'Families and Young People in Troubled Neighbourhoods',
    2 December 2011 (available at: https://www.gov.uk/government/speeches/
    families-and-young-people-in-troubled-neighbourhoods, accessed 16
    March 2017).

41. H. Saul, 'Benefits "Smart Cards" Plan Revealed by Iain Duncan Smith to
    Stop Claimants Spending Welfare Money on Alcohol', *Independent*, 30
    September 2014 (available at: http://www.independent.co.uk/news/uk/
    politics/benefits-smart-cards-plan-revealed-by-iain-duncan-smith-to-
    stop-claimants-spending-welfare-money-on-9763854.html, accessed 30
    November 2016).

42. S.P. Jenkins, 'Poverty Measurement and Within-Household Distribution:
    Agenda for Action', *Journal of Social Policy* 20/4 (1991): 457–483.

43. Millar and Glendinning, 'Gender and Poverty', p. 378.

44. D. Cameron, 'Prime Minister's Speech on Life Chances', 11 January 2016 (available at: https://www.gov.uk/government/speeches/prime-ministers-speech-on-life-chances, accessed 16 March 2017).
45. Ibid.

CHAPTER 7

1. Quoted in J. Welshman, *Underclass: A History of the Excluded Since 1880*, 2nd edn (London: Bloomsbury, 2013), p. 79.
2. Ibid.
3. W. Ryan, *Blaming the Victim* (New York: Vintage, 1971), p. 111.
4. G. Orwell, *The Road to Wigan Pier* [1937] (London: Penguin, 2001), p. 199.
5. There is also increasing evidence of the intervention of the state in the family home through its communications. Kayleigh Garthwaite, a researcher at Durham University, has highlighted the 'fear of the brown envelope' that exists amongst sickness and disability benefit recipients worried about potential changes to their eligibility as a result of government welfare reforms. See K. Garthwaite, 'Fear of the Brown Envelope: Exploring Welfare Reform with Long-Term Sickness Benefits Recipients', *Social Policy and Administration* 48/7 (2014): 782–798.
6. Department for Communities and Local Government (DCLG), 'Working with Troubled Families: A Guide to the Evidence and Good Practice', 2012 (available at: https://www.gov.uk/government/publications/working-with-troubled-families-a-guide-to-evidence-and-good-practice, accessed 16 March 2017), p. 4.
7. Casey has subsequently led other high-profile and controversial work for the government. She was tasked with carrying out an independent review of Rotherham Metropolitan Borough Council in the wake of substantial numbers of children being sexually exploited in the borough, and she also led a review into 'opportunity and integration', published in December 2016, which examined government attempts to improve social cohesion in the UK.
8. L. Casey, 'Speech at Troubled Families Co-ordinators Event', 18 September 2013 (available at: file:///C:/Users/VCNL9/Downloads/TFI%20Coordinators%20event%202013%20(1).pdf, accessed 20 April 2017).
9. House of Commons, 'Oral Evidence Taken before the Communities and Local Government Committee: Community Budgets', uncorrected transcript, 24 June 2013 (available at: http://www.parliament.uk/documents/commons-committees/communities-and-local-government/130624-HC-163-iv-CB-uncorrected-transcript.pdf, accessed 16 March 2017), p. 5.
10. S. Crossley, 'The Troubled Families Programme: In, For and Against the State?' in M. Fenger, J. Hudson and C. Needham (eds), *Social Policy Review 28: Analysis and Debate in Social Policy, 2016* (Bristol: Policy Press, 2016), pp. 127–146.
11. Bristol City Council, 'Troubled Families – One Year On, Edition 1', 12 March 2014 (available at: http://www.voscur.org/system/files/Newsletter%20-%20One%20Year%20On.pdf, accessed 29 November 2016).

12. C. Rosselin, 'The Ins and Outs of the Hall: A Parisien Example', in I. Cieraad (ed.), *At Home: An Anthropology of Domestic Space* (New York: Syracuse University Press, 1999), p. 53.

13. DCLG, 'Working with Troubled Families', p. 6.

14. 'Former Portsmouth Police Officer back on Asbo Beat', *BBC News*, 2 September 2013 (available at: http://www.bbc.co.uk/news/uk-england-hampshire-23896776, accessed 29 November 2016).

15. B. Skeggs, *Class, Self, Culture* (London: Routledge, 2004), p. 113.

16. D. Cameron, 'Speech by Prime Minister David Cameron on Welfare Reform', 25 June 2012 (available at:http://www.telegraph.co.uk/news/politics/david-cameron/9354163/David-Camerons-welfare-speech-in-full.html, accessed 16 March 2017).

17. Bourdieu, 'Social Space and Symbolic Power', p. 17.

18. C. Allan, 'The Extended Benefit Cap Is a Cynical Ploy by the UK Government', *Guardian*, 8 November 2016 (available at: https://www.theguardian.com/society/2016/nov/08/extended-benefit-cap-ploy-exploit-social-division, accessed 29 November 2016).

19. E. Pickles, 'Eric Pickles' Speech to the National Conservation Convention', 5 April 2014 (available at: http://press.conservatives.com/post/82077378511/eric-pickles-speech-to-the-national-conservative, accessed 29 November 2016).

20. Casey, 'Speech'.

21. T. Gold, '"Problem Families" Do Not Need an Army of Hyacinth Buckets Shouting at Them', *Guardian*, 26 August 2011 (available at: https://www.theguardian.com/commentisfree/2011/aug/26/working-families-everything-scheme-tanya-gold, accessed 29 November 2016).

22. J. Deans, 'Jamie Oliver Bemoans Chips, Cheese and Giant TVs of Modern-Day Poverty', *Guardian*, 27 August 2013 (available at: https://www.theguardian.com/lifeandstyle/2013/aug/27/jamie-oliver-chips-cheese-modern-day-poverty, accessed 29 November 2016).

23. A. Collins, 'Poor Show: TV's New Poverty Porn', *Guardian*, 23 August 2013 (available at: https://www.theguardian.com/tv-and-radio/2013/aug/23/tv-poverty-porn, accessed 29 November 2016).

24. D. Cameron, 'Troubled Families Speech', 15 December 2011 (available at: https://www.gov.uk/government/speeches/troubled-families-speech, accessed 13 March 2017).

25. Orwell, *Road to Wigan Pier*, p. 92.

26. Women's Group on Public Welfare, *Our Towns, a Close-Up: A Study Made During 1939–1942* (London: Oxford University Press, 1943), p. 30.

27. Deans, 'Jamie Oliver'.

28. J. Monroe, 'Jamie Oliver Is a "Poverty Tourist"', 28 August 2013 (available at: http://www.iol.co.za/lifestyle/food-drink/food/jamie-oliver-is-a-poverty-tourist-1569386, Accessed 29 November 2016).

29. O. Goldhill, 'Jamie Oliver Says Unhealthy Packed Lunches Are Tantamount to "Child Abuse"', *Independent*, 17 May 2013 (available at: http://www.independent.co.uk/arts-entertainment/tv/news/jamie-oliver-says-

unhealthy-packed-lunches-are-tantamount-to-child-abuse-8621479.html,
accessed 29 November 2016).

30. Quoted from *Jamie's Return to School Dinners* (Fresh One Productions, 2006), broadcast on Channel 4.

31. T. Dalrymple, 'It's Not Poverty That's Fattening – It's the Bad Eating Habits, *Daily Telegraph*, 23 January 2013 (available at: http://www.telegraph.co.uk/news/health/9821278/Its-not-poverty-thats-fattening-its-the-bad-eating-habits.html, accessed 29 November 2016).

32. Ibid.

33. S. Boseley, 'Childhood Obesity: UK's "Inexcusable" Strategy Is Wasted Opportunity, Say Experts', *Guardian*, 18 August 2016 (available at: https://www.theguardian.com/society/2016/aug/18/childhood-obesity-strategy-wasted-opportunity-campaigners, accessed 29 November 2016).

34. Center for Science in the Public Interest, 'Big Food: Sounds a Lot Like Big Tobacco', n.d. (available at: https://cspinet.org/big-food-sounds-lot-big-tobacco, accessed 29 November 2016).

35. Orwell, *Road to Wigan Pier*, p. 55.

36. Women's Group on Public Welfare, *Our Towns*, p. 23.

37. Ryan, *Blaming the Victim*, pp. 86–111.

38. L. Wacquant, *Prisons of Poverty* (Minneapolis: University of Minnesota Press, 2009), p. 12.

39. C. Murray, *Charles Murray and the Underclass: The Developing Debate* (London: IEA, 1996), p. 27.

40. J. Levin, 'The Welfare Queen', *Slate*, 19 December 2013 (available at: http://www.slate.com/articles/news_and_politics/history/2013/12/linda_taylor_welfare_queen_ronald_reagan_made_her_a_notorious_american_villain.html, accessed 29 November 2016).

41. J. Kohler-Hausmann, 'Welfare Crises, Penal Solutions, and the Origins of the "Welfare Queen"', *Journal of Urban History* 41/5 (2015): 756–771.

42. M. Lawson, 'The Making of Blue Peter', *Independent*, 2 April 1994 (available at: http://www.independent.co.uk/arts-entertainment/the-making-of-blue-peter-in-the-last-two-years-peter-lilley-has-shot-from-obscurity-to-euro-baiting-1367591.html, accessed 29 November 2016).

43. I. Tyler, 'Chav Mum, Chav Scum', *Feminist Media Studies* 8/1 (2008): 17–34.

44. Ibid., p. 30.

45. A. Gentleman, 'Troubled Families: "You Need to Do Something Bad before You Get Support"', *Guardian*, 7 April 2013 (available at: https://www.theguardian.com/society/2013/apr/07/troubled-families-support-cameron, accessed 29 November 2016).

46. E. Rathbone, 'Report on the Condition of Widows under the Poor Law in Liverpool' (Liverpool: Lee & Nightingale, 1913), p. 29.

CHAPTER 8

1. D. Cameron, 'Brick by Brick, We're Tearing Down the Big State', *Daily Telegraph*, 28 March 2012 (available at: http://www.telegraph.co.uk/news/

politics/david-cameron/9171481/Brick-by-brick-were-tearing-down-the-big-state.html, accessed 17 March 2017).

2. J. Peck, *Workfare States* (New York: Guilford Press, 2001).

3. Ibid., p. 10, original emphasis.

4. HM Government, 'The Coalition: Our Programme for Government', 2010 (available at: https://www.gov.uk/government/uploads/system/uploads/attachment_data/file/83820/coalition_programme_for_government.pdf, accessed 17 March 2017), p. 8.

5. P. Taylor-Gooby, 'UK Heading for Bottom Place on Public Spending', Poverty and Social Exclusion, n.d. (available at: http://www.poverty.ac.uk/articles-government-cuts-internationalcomparisons-public-spending-whats-new/uk-heading-bottom-place, accessed 3 November 2015).

6. C. Beatty and S. Fothergill, 'The Uneven Impact of Welfare Reform: The Financial Losses to Places and People', Centre for Regional Economic and Social Research, Sheffield Hallam University, 2016 (available at: http://www4.shu.ac.uk/research/cresr/sites/shu.ac.uk/files/welfare-reform-2016.pdf, accessed 15 March 2017).

7. Ibid., p. 3.

8. Ibid.

9. Ibid.

10. D. Innes and G. Tetlow, 'Central Cuts, Local Decision-Making: Changes in Local Government Spending and Revenues in England, 2009–10 to 2014–15', IFS Briefing Note BN166, Institute for Fiscal Studies, 2015 (available at: https://www.ifs.org.uk/uploads/publications/bns/BN166.pdf, accessed 15 March 2017).

11. A. Hastings, N. Bailey, G. Bramley, M. Gannon and D. Watkins, 'The Cost of the Cuts: The Impact On Local Government And Poorer Communities (York: Joseph Rowntree Foundation, 2015), p. 5

12. Innes and Tetlow, 'Central Cuts, Local Decision-Making', p8.

13. N. Puffett, 'More Than 1,000 Children's Centres Axed since 2010', *Children and Young People Now*, 26 April 2016 (available at: http://www.cypnow.co.uk/cyp/news/1156991/more-than-1-000-children-scentres-axed-since-2010?utm_content=&utm_campaign=260416%20Daily%20Bulletin&utm_source=Children%20&%20Young%20People%20Now&utm_medium=adestra_email&utm_term=http://www.cypnow.co.uk/cyp/news/1156991/more-than-1-000-children-s-centres-axed-since-2010, accessed 11 May 2016).

14. See e.g. UNISON, 'The UK's Youth Services: How Cuts Are Removing Opportunities for Young People and Damaging Their Lives', 2014 (available at: https://www.unison.org.uk/content/uploads/2014/07/On-line-Catalogue 225322.pdf, accessed 17 March 2017); and S. Davies, 'The Public Library Service Under Attack: How Cuts Are Putting Individuals and Communities At Risk and Damaging Local Businesses and Economies', 2013 (available at: https://www.unison.org.uk/content/uploads/2013/06/On-line-Catalogue2 15893.pdf, accessed 17 March 2017).

15. J. Harris, 'Save the Library, Lose the Pool: Newcastle Finds Self-Help Has Its Limits as Cuts Bite', *Guardian*, 23 November 2015 (available at: https://www.theguardian.com/business/2015/nov/23/newcastle-cuts-save-library-lose-pool-john-harris, accessed 30 November 2016).

16. H. Pidd, 'Manchester Council Bans Homeless People from Using Library', *Guardian*, 6 May 2015 (available at: https://www.theguardian.com/uk-news/the-northerner/2015/may/06/manchester-council-bans-homeless-people-from-using-library, accessed 30 November 2016).

17. 'Privatising Probation Services Was a Foreseeable Mistake – and Now We All Stand to Pay the Price', *Independent*, 20 December 2015 (available at:http://www.independent.co.uk/voices/privatising-probation-services-was-a-foreseeable-mistake-and-now-we-all-stand-to-pay-the-price-a6780826.html, accessed 17 March 2017).

18. A. Travis, 'Probation Officers Face Redundancy in Plan to Replace Them with Machines', *Guardian*, 30 March 2015 (available at: https://www.theguardian.com/society/2015/mar/30/probation-officers-face-redundancy-in-plan-to-replace-them-with-machines, accessed 30 November 2016).

19. Hastings et al., 'Cost of the Cuts'.

20. Ibid., p. 105.

21. Ibid., p. 50.

22. M. Lipsky, *Street-Level Bureaucracy: Dilemmas of the Individual in Public Services* (New York: Russell Sage, 1980).

23. Ibid., p. 10.

24. F. Fox Piven and R. Cloward, *Poor People's Movements: Why They Succeed, How They Fail* (New York: Pantheon, 1977), p. 20.

25. H. Mulholland, R. Ramesh and P. Walker, 'Boris Johnson Vows to Block "Kosovo-Style Cleansing" of the Poor', *Guardian*, 25 April 2012 (available at: https://www.theguardian.com/society/2012/apr/25/boris-johnson-kosovo-style-cleansing-poor, accessed 30 November 2016).

26. See the Focus E15 website: https://focuse15.org/.

27. 'Over 50,000 Families Shipped Out of London Boroughs in the Past Three Years Due to Welfare Cuts and Soaring Rents', *Independent*, 29 April 2015 (available at: http://www.independent.co.uk/news/uk/home-news/over-50000-families-shipped-out-of-london-in-the-past-three-years-due-to-welfare-cuts-and-soaring-10213854.html, accessed 30 November 2016).

28. P. Butler, 'Benefit Cap Will Hit 116,000 of Poorest Families, Say Experts', *Guardian*, 1 November 2016 (available at: https://www.theguardian.com/society/2016/nov/01/extended-benefit-cap-hit-116000-families-housing-experts, accessed 30 November 2016).

29. P. Bourdieu et al., *The Weight of the World: Social Suffering in Contemporary Society* (Cambridge: Polity Press, 1999), p. 123.

30. L. Wacquant, *Urban Outcasts: A Comparative Sociology of Advanced Marginality* (Cambridge: Polity Press, 2008), p. 83.

31. H. Ferguson, *Child Protection Practice* (Basingstoke: Palgrave Macmillan, 2011).

32. Ibid., p. 20.

33. C. Davies, 'The Health Visitor as Mother's Friend: A Woman's Place in Public Health, 1900–14', *Society for the Social History of Medicine* 1/1 (1988): 39–59.
34. Ibid., pp. 43–44.
35. P. Starkey, The Feckless Mother: Women, Poverty and Social Workers in Wartime and Post-War England', *Women's History Review* 9/3 (2000): 539–557.
36. See the Family Nurse Partnership website: http://fnp.nhs.uk/.
37. Department for Communities and Local Government (DCLG), 'Working with Troubled Families: A Guide to the Evidence and Good Practice', 2012 (available at: https://www.gov.uk/government/publications/working-with-troubled-families-a-guide-to-evidence-and-good-practice, accessed 16 March 2017), p. 21.
38. D. Cameron, 'Troubled Families Speech', 15 December 2011 (available at: https://www.gov.uk/government/speeches/troubled-families-speech, accessed 13 March 2017).
39. L. Casey, 'Former Portsmouth Police Officer Back on ASBO Beat', *BBC News*, 2 September (available at: www.bbc.co.uk/news/uk-england-hampshire-23896776, accessed 11 March 2017).
40. L. Wacquant, 'Crafting the Neoliberal State: Workfare, Prisonfare and Social Insecurity', *Sociological Forum* 25/2 (2010): 197–220.
41. Ibid.
42. E. Higgs, 'The Rise of the Information State: The Development of Central State Surveillance of the Citizen in England, 1500–2000', *Journal of Historical Sociology* 14/2 (2001): 175–197.
43. J. Hudson, 'Digitising the Structures of Government: The UK's Information Age Government Agenda', *Policy and Politics* 30/4 (2000): 515–531.
44. J. Hudson, 'E-galitarianism? The Information Society and New Labour's Repositioning of Welfare', *Critical Social Policy* 23/2 (2003): 268–290.
45. P.M. Garrett, 'Social Work's "Electronic Turn": Notes on the Deployment of Information and Communication Technologies in Social Work with Children and Families', *Critical Social Policy* 25/4 (2005): 529–553.
46. Ibid., pp. 539–540.
47. DCLG, 'Interim Guidance for Troubled Families Programme Early Starter Areas: Sharing Health Information about Patients and Service Users with Troubled Families', 2014 (available at: https://www.staffordshire.gov.uk/community/community/Interim-Guidance-for-troubled-Families-Programme-Early-Starter-Areas.pdf, accessed 17 March 2017).
48. David Webster, a senior research fellow at Glasgow University, has highlighted how over 1 million people on jobseekers' allowance were sanctioned in 2013 alone. A comprehensive list of Webster's briefings on benefits sanctions can be found at: http://www.cpag.org.uk/david-webster (accessed 19 January 2017).
49. P. Neal, 'Troubled Families – Can Technology Help Turn Lives Around?' 27 October 2014 (available at: http://www.capita.co.uk/news-and-opinion/

opinion/2014/can-technology-help-troubled-families.aspx, accessed 3 November 2015).

50. D. McQuillan, 'Algorithmic States of Exception', *European Journal of Cultural Studies* 18/4–5 (2015): 564–576.

51. In Tolkien's *The Lord of the Rings*, a 'palantir' is a magical stone that enables its users to communicate with one another and is capable of seeing things from afar.

52. A. Savva, 'Sunderland Council Builds Big Data Intelligence Hub with Palantir', *ComputerWorld UK*, 16 September 2014 (available at: http://www.computerworlduk.com/data/sunderland-council-builds-big-data-intelligence-hub-with-palantir-3572330/, accessed 30 November 2016).

53. A. Greenberg, 'How a "Deviant" Philosopher Built Palantir, a CIA-Funded Data-Mining Juggernaut', *Forbes*, 14 August 2013 (available at: http://www.forbes.com/sites/andygreenberg/2013/08/14/agent-of-intelligence-how-a-deviant-philosopher-built-palantir-a-cia-funded-data-mining-juggernaut/#12d6ed2a3da8, accessed 30 November 2016).

54. Ibid.

55. R. Mac, 'National Security Darling: Why Condoleezza Rice, David Petraeus and George Tenet Back Palantir', *Forbes*, 29 August 2013 (available at: http://www.forbes.com/sites/ryanmac/2013/08/19/national-security-darling-why-condoleezza-rice-david-petraeus-and-george-tenet-back-palantir/#6295bd591227, accessed 30 November 2016).

56. D. Aitkenhead, 'Troubled Families Head Louise Casey: "What's Missing is Love"', *Guardian*, 29 November 2013 (available at: https://www.theguardian.com/society/2013/nov/29/troubled-families-louise-casey-whats-missing-love, accessed 30 November 2016).

57. Wacquant, 'Crafting the Neoliberal State', p. 210.

CHAPTER 9

1. J.K. Galbraith, *The Age of Uncertainty* (Boston: Houghton Mifflin, 1977), p. 44.

2. A. Schutz and M.G. Sandy, *Collective Action for Social Change: An Introduction to Community Organizing* (New York: Palgrave Macmillan, 2011), p. 19.

3. G.T. Marx, 'Notes on the Discovery, Collection, and Assessment of Hidden and Dirty Data', in J. Schneider and J. Kitsuse (eds), *Studies in the Sociology of Social Problems* (New York: Ablex, 1984), pp. 78–113.

4. P. Bourdieu et al., *The Weight of the World: Social Suffering in Contemporary Society* (Cambridge: Polity Press, 1999), p. 213.

5. Ibid., p. 629.

6. P. Bourdieu, *Sociology in Question* (London: Sage, 1993), p. 269.

7. M. Nicolaus, 'Fat-Cat Sociology: Remarks at the American Sociology Association Convention', 1968 (available at: http://www.colorado.edu/Sociology/gimenez/fatcat.html, accessed 1 December 2016). All quotes in this paragraph are from this source.

8. L. Nader, 'Up the Anthropologist: Perspectives Gained from Studying Up', in D. Hymes (ed.), *Reinventing Anthropology* (New York: Pantheon, 1972), pp. 284–311.
9. A. Sparrow, H. Mulholland, R. Partington and P. Wintour, 'More than 50 MPs Flipped Second Home, New Expenses Figures Show', *Guardian*, 10 December 2009 (available at: https://www.theguardian.com/politics/2009/dec/10/mps-expenses-50-flipped-homes, accessed 22 April 2017).
10. J. Best, 'MPs' Expenses: Top 10 Most Ridiculous Claims Including the £1,600 Duck Island and 55p Horlicks', *Daily Mirror*, 12 September 2013 (available at: http://www.mirror.co.uk/news/uk-news/mps-expenses-top-10-most-2266854, accessed 22 April 2017).
11. Ibid.
12. L. O'Carroll, 'Phone-Hacking Scandal: Timeline', *Guardian*, 24 June 2014 (available at: https://www.theguardian.com/uk-news/2014/jun/24/phone-hacking-scandal-timeline-trial, accessed 22 April 2017).
13. P. Kingsley, 'Financial Crisis: Timeline', *Guardian*, 12 August 2012 (available at https://www.theguardian.com/business/2012/aug/07/credit-crunch-boom-bust-timeline, accessed 22 April 2017).
14. M. Dakers and T. Wallace, 'Libor Scandal: Former City Trader Tom Hayes Gets 14 Years for Rigging Rates' *Daily Telegraph*, 3 August 2015 (available at: http://www.telegraph.co.uk/finance/financial-crime/11767437/Libor-trial-Tom-Hayes-found-guilty-of-rigging-rates.html, accessed 22 April 2017).
15. L. Harding, 'What are the Panama Papers? A Guide to History's Biggest Data Leak', *Guardian*, 5 April 2016 (available at: https://www.theguardian.com/news/2016/apr/03/what-you-need-to-know-about-the-panama-papers, accessed 22 April 2017).
16. D. Boffey, 'Cameron Faces Questions over £200,000 Gift from Mother', *Observer*, 10 April 2016 (available at: https://www.theguardian.com/politics/2016/apr/09/david-cameron-questions-gift-mother, accessed 3 December 2016).
17. D. Pegg, H. Watt, J. Garside and L. Harding, 'Where Does David Cameron's Money Come From? *Guardian*, 6 April 2016 (available at: https://www.theguardian.com/politics/2016/apr/06/the-cameron-network-inherited-wealth-and-family-companies, accessed 3 December 2016).
18. R. Hardy, 'It Was Hard to Stomach David Cameron Preaching Austerity from a Golden Throne', *Guardian*, 13 November 2013 (available at: https://www.theguardian.com/commentisfree/2013/nov/13/david-cameron-austerity-public-sector-cuts, accessed 3 December 2016).
19. J. Robertson, 'Google Tax Row: What's Behind the Deal?' *BBC News*, 28 January 2016 (available at: http://www.bbc.co.uk/news/business-35428966, accessed 3 December 2016).
20. A. Blake, 'Donald Trump's Defenses of Not Paying Taxes Pretty Much Say It All, *Washington Post*, 2 October 2016 (available at: https://www.washingtonpost.com/news/the-fix/wp/2016/09/28/donald-trumps-defense-

of-not-paying-taxes-is-remarkable/?utm_term=.d1c3db059f1f, accessed 3 December 2016).

21. D. Dorling, *Inequality and the 1%* (London: Verso, 2014), p. 5.

22. See e.g. R. Atkinson, 'On the Frontline: Domestic Sovereigns, Wealth and Public Space', Discover Society, 3 December 2013 (available at: http://discoversociety.org/2013/12/03/on-the-frontline-domestic-sovereigns-wealth-and-public-space/, accessed 17 March 2017); and R. Burrows, 'The New Gilded Ghettos: The Geodemographics of the Super-Rich', Discover Society, 3 December 2013 (available at: http://discoversociety.org/2013/12/03/the-new-gilded-ghettos-the-geodemographics-of-the-super-rich/, accessed 17 March 2017).

23. F. Peeraudin, 'Tories Reject Move to Ensure Rented Homes Fit for Human Habitation', *Guardian*, 12 January 2016 (available at: https://www.theguardian.com/society/2016/jan/12/tories-reject-move-to-ensure-rented-homes-fit-for-human-habitation, accessed 4 December 2016).

24. HM Revenue and Customs, 'Measuring Tax Gaps 2016 Edition: Tax Gap Estimates for 2014–15' (available at: https://www.gov.uk/government/uploads/system/uploads/attachment_data/file/561312/HMRC-measuring-tax-gaps-2016.pdf, accessed 3 December 2016).

25. R. Murphy, 'The Tax Gap: Tax Evasion in 2014 – and What Can Be Done about It' (available at: http://www.taxresearch.org.uk/Documents/PCSTaxGap2014.pdf, accessed 3 December 2016).

26. National Audit Office, 'HMRC's Approach to Collecting Tax from High Net Worth Individuals', 2016 (available at: https://www.nao.org.uk/wp-content/uploads/2016/11/HMRCs-approach-to-collecting-tax-from-high-net-worth-individuals.pdf, accessed 17 March 2017).

27. D. Hirsch, 'What Will It Take to End Child Poverty? Firing on All Cylinders' (York: Joseph Rowntree Foundation, 2006).

28. This point is brilliantly made by J. Veit-Wilson, 'Horses for Discourses: Poverty, Purpose and Closure in Minimum Income Standards Policy', in D. Gordon and P. Townsend (eds), *Breadline Europe: The Measurement of Poverty* (Bristol: Policy Press, 2000), pp. 141–164.

29. European poverty statistics are compiled by Eurostat, the statistical office of the European Union. Its poverty statistics can be found at: http://ec.europa.eu/eurostat/web/income-and-living-conditions/statistics-illustrated (accessed 24 January 2017).

30. There is now a wealth of research evidence on the corrosive effects of inequality as well as the inequality between countries: see e.g. Dorling, *Inequality and the 1%*; and the seminal work by R. Wilkinson and K. Pickett, *The Spirit Level: Why Equality is Better for Everyone* (London: Penguin Books, 2010).

31. J. Browne and A. Hood, 'Living Standards, Poverty and Inequality in the UK: 2015–16 to 2020–21', IFS Report R114, 2016 (available at: https://www.ifs.org.uk/uploads/publications/comms/R114.pdf, accessed 20 April 2017).

32. P. Townsend, 'Underclass and Overclass: The Widening Gulf between Social Classes in the 1980s', in M. Cross and G. Payne (eds), *Sociology in Action* (London: Macmillan, 1993), pp. 91–118.
33. Joseph Rowntree Foundation, '100 Questions: Identifying Research Priorities for Poverty Prevention and Reduction' (York: Joseph Rowntree Foundation, 2016).
34. Bourdieu et al., *The Weight of the World*, p. 629.
35. Ibid.
36. C. Ashbaugh, *Lucy Parsons: American Revolutionary* (Chicago: Charles H. Kerr, 1976), p. 266.

Index

Orient, the 7–8
Orwell, George 90, 93
Osborne, George 9–10
Othering
    definition and theory 2–13
    backwardness narratives 15–19, 27,
        32, 35, 40, 51, 114
    culture of poverty concept 16,
        19–21
    imagined lives of the poor 83–97,
        115
    by the media 4–5, 16–22, 23, 24–6,
        30–5, 48, 79, 87, 88–9, 92
    narratives blaming families 3, 10,
        21–8, 59–62, 76–7, 79–82, 86–97,
        106–8, 111–12
    by physical exclusion 37–9, 40, 114
    by politicians 3, 9–10, 22–4, 42–54,
        73–4, 76–82, 93–4
    'sink estates' narratives 42–54,
        61–2, 66
    territorial stigmatisation 5–6, 45,
        46–7, 61, 66, 114
    by Troubled Families Programme
        administrator 85–6, 88, 89–90,
        111
    'workless family' narratives 10, 49,
        73–4, 75–6, 87–8

Pahl, Jan 78
Palantir 110–11
Pearson, Harry 35
Peck, Jamie 98
Persons, Lucy 124
Petonnet, Colette 2–3
photographers, use of poor areas by
    30–2
Pickles, Eric 88
Policy Exchange 36
politicians
    Othering by 3, 9–10, 22–4, 42–54,
        73–4, 76–82, 93–4
    visiting the poor by 13, 42–3,
        49–50, 53
Pontiac Silverdome 31–2
poor doors 38–9

poor people, narratives about see
    Othering
poverty and stigmatisation see
    Othering
poverty porn
    films 30
    photography 30–2
    TV programmes 4, 24–5, 26, 55, 87,
        88–9
    Victorian 16–19
powerful groups and poverty 113–24
private sector 44, 47, 99, 101, 110–11,
    119, 121
probation service privatisation 101
public buildings 103

Radio Times 26
Rathbone, Eleanor 96–7
Reagan, Ronald 93–4
Red Bull video 31
Red Road Flats, Glasgow 37–8
relative poverty 21, 129n41
remasculinisation of the state 107
Requiem for Detroit? (film) 30
researchers, visits to the poor by 4–5,
    12–13, 23–4, 42, 57–68, 125n12
riots (England, 2011) 3, 44, 61
Rosselin, Celine 86
Rowntree, Seebohm 42, 71
Royle Family, The 87
ruin porn 30–4, 39–40
Ryan, William 84, 93

Said, Edward 7–8, 15, 47
schools 13, 54
segregation 37–9, 40, 114
Sheffield Hallam University 54
Shields, Rob 8, 29, 35
Shildrick, Tracy 65
Sibley, David 5, 8–9, 13, 26, 32
Silverdome 31–2
Sims, George 17
single parents 94–5, 99–100
'sink estates' narratives 42–54, 61–2,
    66
sitting rooms, as imagined 87–9